Essentials for Online Business

Quality Information at Your Fingertips

QAIS RAZA

Legal Notice

The Author/Publisher has strived to be as accurate and complete as possible in the creation of this book, notwithstanding the fact that he does not warrant or represent at any time that the contents within are accurate due to the rapidly changing nature of the Internet.

While all attempts have been made to verify information provided in this publication, the Author/Publisher assumes no responsibility for errors, omissions, or contrary interpretation of the subject matter herein. Any perceived slights of specific persons, peoples, or organizations are unintentional.

In practical advice books, like anything else in life, there are no guarantees of income made. Readers are cautioned to reply on their own judgment about their individual circumstances to act accordingly.

This book is not intended for use as a source of legal, business, accounting or financial advice. All readers are advised to seek services of competent professionals in legal, business, accounting, and finance field.

DEDICATION

You can have a great plan, but without support a great team your plan would never have made it from plan to execution. This book is the result of an incredible team of dedicated people who aided, supported, and inspired me to write and ensure readers will do the same.

Many Thanks to family (My Grand Mother, Father, Mother, Brothers and specially my loving wife, Rubina Hasnain– my constant source of strength and most honest critic), friends, clients, and colleagues.

AKNOWLEDGEMENTS

To all who have directly or indirectly contributed to the making of this book.

CONTENTS

Acknowledgments   i

1 Leaverage   1

Group Leaverage   1

Joint Venture Marketing Leaverage   1

Traffic Leaverage   3

Safe Rule of Thumb for any Business Endeavor   4

Labor Replication   5

Due Diligence   6

One Chance on the Merry-Go-Round of Life   8

2 You are your Target Audience   9

What is in for Me?   9

Compelling Copy   10

Delivery is Everything   14

Getting Your Reader's Attention   14

Honing Your Copy Writing Skills   17

Practice   19

The Naked Truth   19

Personalise and Be Specific   22

In Review   28

3 Affiliate Marketing   31

   How To Get Started   31

   Earning Potential   35

4 YouTube   37

   How To Get Started   37

   Earning Potential   43

5 Blogging   44

   Introduction To Online Journaling   44

   How Can Blogging Be Profitable To Individual? 47

   How To Get Started   50

   Earning Potential   54

   Getting Constant Traffic To Your Blog   55

6 Google AdSense A-To-Z   59

   3 Reasons Why AdSense Is Essential   61

   How To Start Making Money With AdSense   64

   5 Ways To Improve Your AdSense Earnings   66

   Monetising Your Website With AdSense   69

   What Is It That They Are Doing Wrong?   72

Increase Your AdSense Cash   74

Avoid Getting Your Account Terminated   76

7   Freelancer   80

How To Get Started   80

Earning Potential   84

8   Selling Physical Products Online   85

How To Get Started   85

9   e-Commerce   92

How To Get Started   94

10   Dropshipping   98

Five Golden Rules to Dropshipping   100

Reasons for Starting a Dropshipping Business   102

Things to Consider   104

The Advantages and Disadvantages   107

How to get Started   110

PREFACE

Are you looking for a way to make more money, but don't want to go out and get another job? Would you like to learn how to increase your income by working online, straight from the comforts of your home, possibly without even getting out of your pajamas? If you answered yes to either (or both) of these questions, you are in the right place.

You probably already know that there are many ways to obtain what you want financially, because others have found them and profited from them tremendously already. You just need a little direction in your search. You need someone to tell you what options are available to you and how to get started with them and that is where this book comes in.

In it, you will learn ten different techniques to make money online (some of which contain several options within them). A few of them may take a while to learn and perfect, but others you can start using today, potentially earning you more income by the time the clock strikes midnight tonight.

What you are about to learn in the pages and chapters ahead is ten different techniques to make money with nothing more than an Internet connection and a will to get out of your current financial situation. While this list is certainly not all inclusive, it will give you an idea of the most popular
Internet-based ways of making money available to you today.

In the end, it is up to you how profitable you are with any of these suggestions. You can make nothing or you can make a million dollars. Your ability to succeed is based on your ingenuity, creativity, ability to reach your target market, and unwavering perseverance. As long as you continue to learn from your mistakes, perfect your steps, and choose to do the best you can, then you will win in the end.

1 LEVERAGE

GROUP LEVERAGE

Like a long pole, that can shift a great weight with little effort; such is the case with succeeding in business.

Your chances of succeeding- as an 'army of one' fall somewhere between zip, zilch and nill.

Social Marketing [i.e. Joint Venture Marketing] is the critical key to enjoying on-going success. There are approximate 100,000,000+ Web sites out there...and growing daily.

Without some good old' fashion Joint Venture Networking skills under your belt; you chances of *not* getting noticed are virtually guaranteed! Though there are many different types of leverage, two- in particular- will be explored in this segment:

JOINT VENTURE MARKETING LEVERAGE

All but gone [certainly rare, to say the least] are the days when you could merely just e-mail an E-zine Publisher with a copy of your offerings and a 50% profit-share.

You've got to captivate your potential Joint Venture Partners with a more strategic, longer-range heap of killer benefits, as well. Prove to them that you are extremely sensitive to *their* overall wants, needs and desires- not yours or mine.

Good Strategic Joint Venture Alliances take time to cultivate...It's all about building trust.

When a List Master recognizes you as a genuine Expert within your niche, and that you just don't recommend anything that you- yourself- are not absolutely delighted with as the end-consumer...

They will be far more enthusiastic about JV'ing with you in the future, because people like to do business with people they know and trust...

- ☐ Are you someone who is trustworthy and whole-heartedly worth getting to know?

- ☐ Does your JV Proposal showcase *them* in the 'limelight'?

- ☐ Is your focus on assisting them, in every way within your means, to help them grow their business and become even more successful?

If not- You need to seriously reconsider your marketing priorities...before you 'figure it out' the hard way!

That said...nothing can propel you to [seemingly] overnight

success like a well-thought-out and deftly-crafted JV-Nothing.

Every single truly successful marketer realized- at some point within their career- that in order to get to where their truly trying to be; they have to whole-heartedly and cheerfully assist others in doing the same.

This is especially true when making first contact with a good potential Partner...remember; it is you going to them, for something you want- Not the other way around.

Until you've cultivate your own Master List of 20,000, 50,000, even 100,000 Loyal Readers; and you are now the one getting slammed with 10 to 20 Joint Venture Proposals per day, on average...

To create successful, mutually beneficial JV's; you must pole-position your wants, needs and desires in such a way as to naturally resonate with/compliment theirs.

Often times, this is *much* easier said than done; as good JV Proposals require a fair and reasonable amount of selfless and candid receptiveness, attention to detail and deep meditation.

However...the dividends are supremely worth it!

TRAFFIC LEVERAGE

Short of having a 'bottomless wallet'...you will quickly realize, early in your online success endeavors; exactly just how difficult it is to drive consistent, quality traffic to your Web site.

Virtually all of the 'marketing gurus' trying to sell you how you, too, can quickly and easily make boatloads of cash online, with no out of pocket expenses; are feeding you a fat, stinky pile o' bull. Run...Fast!

And hide your wallet!!!

Furthermore, they straight-up buy their traffic, one way or another; until such point as they have established a monster downline of resellers [one of your primary goals, actually].

Ahhh, yes...

Then you too can- indeed- make boatloads of cash on the Internet and perhaps even become the next 'guru'...

SAFE RULE OF THUMB FOR ANY BUSINESS ENDEAVOR

The more money [up front] you invest in yourself, the less time that you'll be shackled to your venture. The less money you are willing to you invest in yourself, the more time you will spend [exponentially] to overcome lack of funds.

In a nutshell, you can actually become quite successful on the Internet- generating a modest four figures a month- with virtually no out-of-pocket expenses. However...

Do plan on exercising Due Diligence and spending thousands of hours.

Hence, why it is critically important to choose something that you are 100% *absolutely* passionate about- as the end-consumer hobbyist!

I apologize if the blunt truth of the matter 'takes the wind out of your sails'...but, again- I wish someone was this brutally honest with me years ago!

"This will increase your profitability substantially, while cutting down your work load!"

LABOR REPLICATION

The closer you want to get to all of that free time and boatloads of money you've indubitably been promised time and time again...

The more closely you must examine exactly what it takes to become as digitally automated as possible! Which also takes into consideration creative opportunities such as outsourcing, viral e-marketing and B2B JV barter.

One very excellent example is the awe-inspiring power of autoresponders. Depending on your particular approach; a deftly-crafted autoresponder series can cultivate long-term customers, clients, subscribers, etc...Only if the information you are divulging high-quality.

Another prime example is a genuinely high-quality, PLR e-book. Most especially if these can be re-branded, featuring your downlines' primary Web venture.

Perhaps a Strategic Joint Venture Alliance...or a Member Site- In which you provide your members with a step-by-step plan of action and everything they need to achieve their own success, on- line [tenacity notwithstanding, of course]!

In each of these examples, the Principle of Labor Replication [another demonstration of leverage] is invoked- your one and only Way to *consistent* Internet Success-

Regardless of your offerings...but if you are not willing to actually put forth the effort and initially act upon your knowledge, and then this will merely be entertainment to you.

DUE DILIGENCE

This is one subject that the vast majority of Internet Marketing 'gurus' avoid like the plague.

Why?

Because if they were 100% straight-up with you from the get-go and told you in no uncertain detail exactly just how hard, time-consuming and resource-consuming owning and operating your own truly successful biz op *really* is...

They somehow got it figured that you'll end up opting out and they'll end up losing the almighty buck they stood to make on your complete and utter ignorance. The faster and easier they promise you tons of money and leads; the far more cynical I'd be, if I were you.

And this applies to the so-called Joint Venture Systems out there, as well-of which I own several.

Good, solid long-lasting Joint Ventures actually do require a great deal of time, effort and giving of yourself...especially if they require a Joint Venture Agreement Contract.

However- these are the very the types of JV's that really can make you fabulously wealthy... seemingly overnight.

As a matter of fact, if it is anything short of a methodically built-up System- over a reasonable period of time [6 months to a year]...then I can all but guarantee you that you are setting yourself up for some serious grief.

Sure...the rare exception to the rule- such as that deftly-crafted and patiently-researched Joint Venture Proposal you hit BIG with in just a few short weeks or even days...because you done paid your Due Diligence!

An entirely different approach: Tell your people the *whole* truth- and nothing but.

Don't sell them pipe dreams, fluff and just plain crap; in the hope of making a sale. In fact, don't sell them anything. Give 'Till It Hurts [for being such a blatantly promiscuous sneezer...it happens to be one of Robert G. Allen's truly superb Principles].

And when you actually do attempt to 'sell' your reader something:

Do it in a way that they are both absolutely eager and confident in your recommending them such a kick@$$deal, offer, etc. Treat your Reader [most literally] as if they were your best friend, and develop a relationship accordingly. And this is just one of many ways Due Diligence comes into play.

One very sad mistake made over and over again -particular to Internet Marketing proselytes and neophytes- is promotion of a cookie-cutter biz op that they are absolutely not the delighted end user of. Self-evident.

If you're just starting out [or strongly considering doing so] - Do not fall into this fatal trap....

In other words, before you go wishing failure, stress and duress upon yourself...

Compliments of the infamous University of Hard Knocks:

"Be the end consumer of whatever it is you'd seriously consider promoting, and put it to the hardest-core Satisfaction Tests that you can possibly devise."

ONE CHANCE ON THE MERRY-GO-ROUND OF LIFE

Find a means of online revenue that is something you are already approaching as a joyful leisure hobby; and then research out biz ops that naturally compliment your favorite hobby.

After carefully researching and refining your biz op you'd like to focus on; aggressively put it to the test- as the end user- and see if it truly stands and [over-] Delivers on all Promises made.

And, though this may- at first- sound a bit oxymoronic; do NOT focus on making the sale. Instead, focus on the wants, needs and desires of your Loyal Readership, and sales will follow in a completely relaxed, zero-pressure manner.

Your Readers will appreciate your lack of hype and high-pressure sales tactics; and will be quicker to recommend you [provided you freely quality content with them]!

2 YOU ARE YOUR TARGET AUDIENCE

WHAT'S IN IT FOR ME?

It's ALL about value adding. If I were to actually take a moment out of my busy day, and experience your Web endeavor for the first time...

"The challenge you face is that people don't care about you. They care about themselves, which is pretty natural."

- Seth Godin

Flipping the Funnel [Companies Edition]

☐ What is my very first impression, visually, of your site?

☐ Are you using obnoxious/psychotic color schemes, hard-to-read fonts and/or multi-media over-load...

☐ Or, is your page clean, crisp and completely devoid of truly unnecessary noise and clutter?

☐ Is your color/font scheme aesthetically pleasing to the eye?

☐ Does your layout represent single-focus, which a clear and definitive call to action?

☐ What real value are you actually adding to me?

☐ Does the amount of value {you seek to add to me} inspire me to naturally share your Web site with others, based on simple excellence?

☐ Can you actively pinpoint each of the viral techniques both present, and missing, in each of your Web endeavors?

This one Principle, alone- if mastered with passion and zeal-will conservatively increase your base-rate chances of outstanding success by at least double.

Do NOT, for love of all that is precious in your life, promote something that you are not whole-heartedly sold on- as the end-user: failure is a statistical certainty waiting to happen.

COMPELLING COPY

Thousands of books have been written on the subject and more are being manufactured daily... A subject that most people have a difficult time- at best- to actually sit down and learn just the fundamentals of.

And with good reason...it's Real Work.

However, you will be simply astounded -if not outright floored- when you pay your Due Diligence and see just how much per hour top Sales Copy writers are thoroughly enjoying-

And they can easily command these prices because the amount of people that actually can write juicy, hypnotic copy are very far and exceptionally few in between...

People like Henry Gold, Brett McFall and Alex Mandossian. Is yours up to snuff?

Remember the Great Internet Marketing Caveat: Your Web, sales, and autoresponder copy.

Why?

There's a whole lot of it out there that comes across as just plain cheesy. Pay your due diligence and start your own private swap file of both on and off line ads/sales copy that:

☐   Totally grabs you, or...
    ☐
☐   Leaves you with the impression that a chimpanzee would most likely have created a better ad or superior sales copy!

The former is to inspire you to write your own compelling sales copy [not to plagiarize, of course]...while the latter is to inspire you to see all advertising in a whole new light...

Whether it be radio, TV, Web, etc.

Specifically- how you would make a bad ad or sales copy

compelling; and really compelling sales/JV copy or ads irresistible. Take some time each and every day to gain further mastery in copy writing. In as few as a few short months- even weeks-

You'll find yourself able to quickly and easily adapt to [and emulate] quite a number of different writing styles and 'voices'. Furthermore, you will start to naturally pick ads and copy apart and 'rebuild' them...almost subconsciously.

When that happens, compelling copy will begin to flow out of you like a refreshing babbling brook!

Just imagine the untold money you'll save, alone, writing your own copy...and money saved is money earned...not to mention the fact that you'll be cultivating a high-paying skill in huge demand.

The best part, however, is the fact that you do not have to rely on someone else's concept of 'good' copy- heck, you'll be quickly designing your own in practically no time!

If the extent of your effort is merely to present your offerings in a bland, uninteresting way-

Then whether or not you actually make the sale depends solely on your price, and the visual information I can glean from the quality of your photos.

If I actually, really want your offering bad enough, I might convince myself to send you an e-mail with a question or two.

However, that detracts from both my precious time and overall eBay experience- unless I want your item THAT bad; which I most seriously doubt- all things being what they are.

Let's face it- we live much harried lives with a bazillion "taxing" of our extremely limited time and money resources.

If you do not inspire me to keep reading- for my own personal enjoyment- you have a better than a99% chance of losing my- and countless other's- interest and business.

Why? With just eBay, alone, I have millions of consumer choices at my immediate fingertips. And that doesn't even factor in the other 70+ million Web Sites, my bills, children's needs, etc., etc.!!!

However, when you inject your personality into your descriptions and storefront, and it's one I find somewhat intriguing; at very least- you'll inspire me to read on a little farther.

Maybe put your site in my fave's, to get back to. Perhaps your Character even persuaded me to make a modest bid! One thing's for absolute certain, though- you will sell far more, far quicker, by putting some real personality into your copy! Remember...

The globalize attention span is about as long as the average cell phone antenna.

With a little bit of extra time invested- you may very easily find your sales doubling, tripling even quadrupling; far greater than what they would have been...if you would've just "let happen as it may"...test, Test, TEST!

The primary way the world will know you is by your copy; convince us you're worth knowing- because you get one shot- and friends do business with friends, over strangers!

DELIVERY IS EVERYTHING

"It doesn't matter whether your product is information or a flyswatter. If you understand marketing, you can make serious income."

Robert G. Allan, Author

Multiple Streams of Internet Income

How will your offerings make me look better, feel better? What will my family and friends say? Will this help me enjoy my leisure? Money is forever the great desire.

Saving money and buying at a lower price are sound copy points. But they must be followed through with benefits, reasons, sound facts and lots more benefits.

When designing your copy, stick to the emotionally-gratifying benefits. A potential customer may be sold, but will that person buy?

GETTING YOUR READER'S ATTENTION

Endorsements and testimonials are effective ways to dramatize facts and back up the benefits of your product, but don't use ones that look or feel transparent- bad juju.

If you use an endorsement from a famous or popular person, that person should use the product. Any testimonials you use must be true. Always aim for satisfaction. Self-respect, accomplishment and security are human aspects everyone strives for.

Never talk down to the readers as though you know

something they don't or you're better than they are. To you, the potential customer is POTENTIAL GOLD.

- 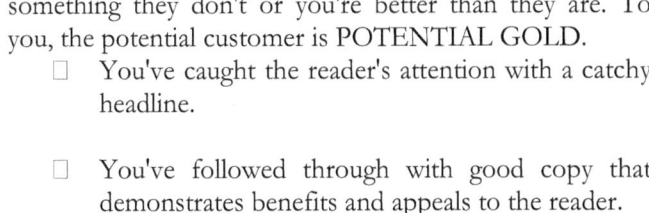 You've caught the reader's attention with a catchy headline.

- You've followed through with good copy that demonstrates benefits and appeals to the reader.

Now- before you lose that interest -command an action in their baser interests [greed, sloth, etc...

You can to close the gap between reading your sales copy and acting upon impulse. The purpose of your eBay ad is to make people buy. You have to tighten the desire to buy.

An iron-clad money-back guarantee is the most useful tool in pressing action-
The more generous, the better! It goes for the bottom line: What do I have to lose?

And it affirms the quality of the product. If you are willing to back the claims you make with a full refund, you can get a hook into those borderline buyers.

Absolutely STAND BEHIND your word. Be cheerful and expedient in returning a refund. Let them know that you sincerely appreciate their business and not to hesitate in contacting you, if there is any way you can be of further assistance.

If you give a time limit the product will be offered for sale, or mention a limited supply, or have a reduced price for a certain time, you'll increase the impulse to act.

Again, STAND BEHIND your word; do not make a "time sensitive" or limited quantity offer that- in fact- is not; illegal and unethical- better to be a flaming spammer!

What you're after...

- Appeal to the reader's urgency;

- Make the product totally irresistible to have- now;

- Extend a generous guarantee;

- Whole-heartedly stand behind the above!

What is your competition doing? When testing new ads; start with the tried and true. Don't try to be different. It is the sound and worthwhile that brings in the customers- time and time again.

The best way to write your ad is to disregard size at first, writing everything on paper that might attract readers.

Tell it all. Stress the need for what you have to offer, what it will do for readers, how they will benefit, benefit and benefit, what they can expect by using your product, how easy or more pleasant life will be for them...

When you have finished writing, you might have a long paragraph or a dozen pages. Now is the time to think of clarity, not cost. Unlike a 'zine classified, you do not pay by the word.

So you won't have to be nearly as selective in your choice of words in the final ad.

To build sales, this advertising must be seen or heard by potential buyers, and cause them to react to the advertising in some way. The credit for the success, or the blame for the failure of almost all ads, reverts back to the ad itself.

The bottom line in any ad is quite simple: To make the reader buy the product or service.

Any ad that causes the reader to only pause in this thinking, to just admire the product, or to simply believe what's written about the product -is not doing its job completely.

The "ad writer" must know exactly what he wants his reader to do, and any that does not elicit the desired action is an absolute waste of time and money.

Never forget the basic rule of advertising copy writing:

"If the ad is not read, it won't stimulate any sale; if it is not seen, it cannot be read; and if it does not command or grab the attention of the reader, it will not be seen!"

Most successful advertising copywriters know these fundamentals backwards and forwards.

Whether you know them already or you're just now being exposed to them...

Your knowledge and practice of these fundamentals will determine the extent of your success as an advertising copywriter.

All Web copy, sales copy and ads are written according to all the same rules. What is said in a 'zine classified ad must have the same [if not more] impact that's delivered in a larger, more elaborate type of Web site, in ultra-condensed form.

HONING YOUR COPY WRITING SKILLS

To start learning how to write good ads, carefully study:

- ☐ High-octane Copy Writers, like Marc Goldmanand Alex Mandossian.

- ☐ Issues of The National Enquirer. These are some of the all-time highest paid copy writers, and with good reason- sales of products advertised.

No, I am not suggesting studying articles such as "Jennifer Williams Gets Impregnated By Alien!". Only the ads.

Analyze each of these ads for the following:

- ☐ How has the writer attracted your attention

- ☐ What about the ads keeps your interest?

- ☐ Are you stimulated to want to know more about the product being advertised?

- ☐ What action must you take?

- ☐ How strongly are you "turned on" by each of these ads?

Rate these ads on a scale of one to ten, with ten being the best. Now, just for practice- without clipping the ads- do the same thing with ten different ads from a Wards or Penney's catalog.

In fact, every ad you see form now on, quickly analyze it, and rate it somewhere on your scale.

If you'll practice this exercise on a regular basis, you'll soon be able to quickly recognize the "Power Points" of any ad you see, and know within your own mind whether an ad is good, bad or otherwise, and what makes it so.

This will give you the "feel" of the fundamentals and style necessary in writing successful ads.

It takes dedicated and regular practice, but you can do it!

Simply recognize and understand the Master Formula [A.I.D.A.]:

☐   Attention!
☐   Interest!
☐   Desire!
☐   Action!

PRACTICE

Practice reading and writing the good ads -and rewriting the bad ones to make them better- and keep at it...until the Formula, the Idea, and the feel of this kind of ad writing becomes second nature to you.

This is the ONLY WAY to gain expertise in writing good copy, including classified ads.

Virtually all successful copywriters rate the headline and/or the lead sentence of an ad as the most important part of the ad, and in reality, you should do the same.

After all, when you ad is surrounded by hundreds of other auction ads; what makes you think anyone is going to see your particular ad?

This brings you to...

THE NAKED TRUTH

The truth is, they're not going to see your ad unless you can immediately reach out and grab their attention; entice them to read all of what you have to say.

Your headline has to make it more difficult for your prospect to ignore or pass over, than to stop and read your ad. If you don't capture the attention of your reader with your headline, anything beyond is useless effort and wasted money.

Successful advertising headlines- are written as promises, either implied or direct.

The former promises to show you how to save money, make money, or attain a desired goal. The latter is a warning against something undesirable.

Example of a Promise: Are You Ready To Become A Millionaire -In Just 18 Months?

Example of a Warning: Do You Make These Mistakes In English?

In both of these examples, I've posed a question as the headline. Headlines that ask a question seem to attract the reader's attention almost as surely as a moth is drawn to a flame.

Once she's seen the question, she just can't seem to keep himself from reading into the rest of the ad to find out the answer.

Remember, however, that your first 250 words are going to make or break whether they read on- and usually a lot less than that!

The best headline questions are those that challenge the reader; that involve her self-esteem, and do not allow her to dismiss your question with a simple yes or no.

You'll be the envy of your friends is another kind of "reader appeal" to incorporate into your headline whenever appropriate.

The appeal has to do with basic psychology: everyone wants to be well thought of, and consequently, will read into the body of your ad to find out how she can gain the respect and accolades of her friends.

Wherever and whenever possible, use colloquialisms or words that are not usually found in advertisements. The idea is to shock or shake the reader out of his reverie and cause him to take notice of your ad.

Most of the headlines you see day in and day out, have certain sameness with just the words rearranged.

The reader may see these headlines with his eyes, but his brain fails to focus on any of them because there's nothing different or out of the ordinary to arrest his attention.

Example of Colloquialism: Do You Experience Severe Brain Farts?

Another attention-grabber kind of headline is the comparative priced magazine headline: Three For Only $3, Regularly $3 Each!

Still another of the tried and proven kind of headlines is the specific question: Do You Suffer From These Symptoms??? And of course, if you offer a strong guarantee, you should say so in your headline: Your Money Refunded, If You Don't Make $100,00 Your First Year.

How To headlines have a very strong basic appeal, but in some instances, they're better used as book titles than advertising headlines.

Who Else Wants In On The Finer Things -which your product or service presumably offers- is another approach with a very strong reader appeal. The psychology here is the need of everyone to belong to a group (read herd mentality)- complete with status and prestige motivations.

Whenever, and as often as you can naturally work it in, you should use the word "you" (and its derivatives) in your headline, and throughout your copy.

After all, your ad should be directed to "one" person, and the person reading your ad wants to feel that you're talking to her personally, not everyone who lives on her street.

PERSONALISE AND BE SPECIFIC

Whenever you sit down to write advertising copy intended to pull the orders -sell the product -you should picture yourself in a one-on-one situation and "talk" to your reader just as if you were sitting across from him at your dining room table.

Be specific and ask him if these are the things that bother him -are these the things he wants -and he's the one you want to buy the product...the layout you devise for your ad, or the frame you build around it, should also command attention.

Either make it so spectacular that it stands out like lobster at a chili dinner, or so uncommonly simple that it catches the reader's eye because of its very simplicity [known as a "plain vanilla" Web site].

It's also important that you don't get cute with a lot of unrelated graphics and other "eye candy". Your ad should convey the feeling of excitement and movement, but should not tire the eyes or disrupt the flow of the message you are trying to present.

Any graphics or artwork you use should be relevant to your product, its use and/or the copy you have written about it. Graphics [other than your product photo] should be used modestly- as artistic touches; to create an atmosphere.

Any photos within your ad should complement the selling of your product, and prove or substantiate specific points in your copy. Once you have your reader's attention, the only way you are going to keep it, is by quickly and emphatically telling him what your product will do for him.

Your potential buyer doesn't care in the least how long it's taken you to produce the product, how long you have been in business, nor how many years you've spend learning your craft- save that for you About Me page for those who are interested!

All she really wants to know, is specifically how she is going to benefit from the purchase of your product. Period. Generally, her wants (and perceived needs) will fall into one of the following categories:

☐ Better health;

☐ More comfort;

☐   More money;

☐   More leisure time;

☐   More popularity;

☐   Greater charisma/beauty;

☐   Greater success and/or

☐   Greater security!

Even though you have your reader's attention, you must follow through with an enthusiastic enumeration of the benefits you can gain. In essence, you must reiterate the advantages, comfort and happiness she'll enjoy -as you have implied in your headline.

Mentally picture your prospect -determine his wants and emotional needs -put yourself in his shoes, and ask yourself: If I were reading this ad, what are the things that would appeal to me?

Write your copy to appeal to your reader's wants, emotional needs and ego cravings!

Remember, it's not the "safety features" that have sold fine cars for the past 50 years -nor has it been the need of transportation. It has been, and almost certainly always will be the advertising writer's recognition of people's wants and emotional/ego needs/cravings.

Visualize your prospect, recognize his wants and satisfy them. Then Stand and Deliver on your promise, with a sweet, unadvertised bonus bundle!

Writing good advertising copy is nothing more or less than

knowing "who" your buyers are; recognizing what he wants; and then telling him how your product will fulfill each of those wants.

"I can define copy writing in two words: applied psychology."

- Alex Mandossian

The "desire" portions of your ad is where you present the facts of your product; create and justify your prospect's conviction, and cause her to demand "a piece of the action" for herself.

It's vitally necessary that you present "proven facts" about your product because survey results show that at least 80% of the people reading your ad -especially those reading it for the first time -will tend to question its authenticity.

So, the more facts you can present in the ad, the more credible your offer. People want "logical facts" to justify emotional surges of instant gratification- as reasons/excuses for buying a product.

It's like the girl who wants to marry the guy her father calls a "no good bum."

Her heart -her emotions- tell her yes, but she needs to nullify the seed of doubt lingering in her mind- to rationalize her decision to go on with the wedding.

In other words, the "desire" portion of your ad has to build belief and credibility in the mind of your prospect.

It has to assure him of his good judgment in the final decision to buy- furnish evidence of the benefits you have promised- and afford him a "safety net" in case anyone should question his decision to buy.

People tend to believe the things that appeal to their ego, individual desires, fears and other emotions. Once you have established a belief in this manner, logic and reasoning are used to support it. Your reader "wants" to believe your ad if she has read it through this far-

It is up to you to support her initial desire.

Study your product and everything about it- visualize the wants of your prospective buyers- dig up the facts, and you'll almost always find plenty of facts to support the buyer's reasons for buying.

Here is where you use results of tests conducted, growing sales figures to prove increasing popularity, and "user" testimonials or endorsements.

"Just exactly what is it for me?!?"

Draw a mental picture for your potential buyer. Let her imagine owning the product. Induce her to visualize all of the benefits you have promised. Give her the keys to seeing herself richer, enjoying luxury, having time to do whatever she would like to do, and with all of her dreams fulfilled.

This can be handled in one or two sentences, or spelled out in a paragraph or more, but it is the absolute ingredient you must include prior to closing the sale. Study all the enticing sales presentations you have ever heard; look at every winning ad; these are the elements that actually make the sales for you.

Remember them, use them, and don't try to sell anything without them. Lots of ads are beautiful, almost perfectly written, and quite convincing- yet they fail to command action form the reader. If you want the reader to have your product, then tell her so and command that she send her money now.

Unless you enjoy spending money on eBay listings, mildly entertaining your prospects with your beautiful writing skills; always command that she complete the sale now, by taking action now- by ordering, visiting your eBay store or Web site, etc.

Once you have got her on the hook- land her! Don't let her get away!

Probably, one of the most common and best methods of moving the reader to act now, is written in some form of the following:

- ☐ All of this can be yours!

- ☐ You can start enjoying this new way of life immediately, simply by sending a check for $XX!

- ☐ Don't put it off, then later wish you had gotten in on the ground floor!

- ☐ Make out that check now, and "be IN on the ground floor!"

- ☐ Act now, and as an "early-bird" buyer, we'll include a big bonus package -absolutely free, simply for acting immediately!

- ☐ You win all the way!

- ☐ We take all the risk!

☐ If you are not satisfied, simply return the product and we will quickly refund your money!

☐ Do it now!

☐ Get that check on its way to us today, and receive the big bonus package!

☐ After next week, we won't be able to include the bonus as a part of this fantastic deal, so act now!

☐ The sooner you act, you more you win!

IN REVIEW

Mastering the fundamentals of Social Networking and the Web2.0 philosophy is merely the permission-based art of selling- knowing how to present whatever it is that you're selling to your visitor in such a manner that she feels you will personally solve her problems or fulfill her dreams.

Anybody can sell anything to anybody and selling on the Web- absolutely no different than selling by mail, in person, or face to face with your prospect...just a more efficient and economical way of making contact:

☐ You've got to captivate her attention;

☐ You've got to appeal to her interests;

☐ You've got to reveal to her how her purchase of your product will benefit her;

☐ You've got to close the sale by causing her to reach into her purse for her credit card or to write out a check for whatever it is you're selling.

The first few seconds of the opening encounter with your prospect ultimately affects the success of the presentation and inevitably-whether or not a sale is made. Therefore, it's absolutely critical that your sales presentation radiates enthusiasm and success!

Once she's on your Site and is looking at your presentation, you've got to make her feel comfortable; be friendly and believable. Stimulate her interest in whatever you're selling by appealing to one of her primordial wants, needs or problems with a solution.

Don't waste her time with a long and/or complicated dissertation...

☐ Make your sales presentation flow;

☐ Anticipate her objections;

☐ Logically answer them within your presentation.

☐ Explain all of the irresistible benefits gained from ownership of your product or service;

☐ Whenever possible, let her see or read of proof or testimonials from people who have already bought from you.

The most important thing you want to do is to create-within your presentation- the fulfillment she'll have as a result of buying from you....

☐ Stimulate her imagination;

☐ Explain to her how she can use whatever you're selling to solve her problems or achieve her dreams;

☐ Invite her to attend the theater of her own mind;

☐

☐ Cast a word movie that allows her to see herself ultimately gratified and satisfied with your product.

☐ Give her a payment button to click on or a simple benefits-packed squeeze page.

☐ Make it as simple and as easy as possible for your prospect to buy from you, extend a generous guarantee and – most importantly- STAND BEHIND IT.

The payment button, order agreement or simple coupon should close the sale for you - that is, if your presentation is well-written and highly compelling; she sees what you're selling as an immediate solution to one of her immediate wants, needs or problems!

Too many sites begin with some sort of blah-blah story about the seller...

"Hello there, I'm writing to you from the beautiful beaches of Waikiki" Or...

"After a hundred years of research I've found the fountain of youth".

Even some such tripe as "dear friend, you may not know me but I'm now a millionaire..." blah biddy blah.

Just ask them if they'd like to _____ ...if so, let me explain; if not, then I don't want to waste your time. Treat your prospects as though their time is more precious than your own!

3 AFFILIATE MARKETING

The first, and perhaps most well-known online money making strategy is called affiliate marketing. It is the most important method of making money online, because you can combine it with almost any of the other methods that are in this book. Affiliate marketing involves selling other people's products or services on your website, social media page, YouTube account, and other Internet-based pages, thereby earning a commission on each sale.

Of course, this money making option requires that you have (or create) an Internet site or page and that site or page caters to the same market as the merchant or advertiser that you want to highlight and you should also have enough visitors. But once you have that, you could make   some   serious   cash.

HOW TO GET STARTED

If the idea of affiliate marketing interests you, here is a quick step-by-step guide to getting you started:

Step #1:

Select the category you wish to promote. This is pretty easy to do if you already have an existing site or page, as it is going to be one that is relevant to your subject or topic. For instance, if you currently own and operate a website that is somehow related to money or financial issues, you could increase your income base as an affiliate marketer (in which you would be called the publisher) by promoting and selling products and programs related to this topic (like the programs sold by Dave Ramsey, creator of Financial Peace University, or Jim Cramer, host of Mad Money).

However, if you don't have a page or site set up currently, what types of products or services are you interested in? What are some things that you are knowledgeable about and can discuss intelligently with your readers? Select a category that you love or could add value to and the rest of the process will be much easier for you.

Step #2:

Set up a site or web page if you don't currently have one. If you don't already have a website or page set up, now is the time to do it. Some options to consider include developing a price comparison site, crafting a review site, or making a discount site for products that people commonly buy online as each one has the ability to attract consumers looking for specific items. Also, sites like these serve a functional purpose for the consumer; whether it is to help them save money, figure out which products are higher qualities, or both, while putting more money in your pocket at the same time.

Step #3:

Decide what products or services you want to promote. If you don't believe in the product or service that you are an affiliate for, how can you expect your reader to be?

Think of the items that you have no problem recommending to your closest family and friends and your passion for them will shine through more clearly, getting your reader as excited about them as you are.

Step #4:

Pick which affiliate marketing site(s) you'd like to use and set up an account. If you're new to affiliate marketing, you may want to check out sites such as Click bank, Amazon Affiliate Programs, E- Junkie, Pay Dotcom (which pays commissions via PayPal), and CJ Affiliate by Conversant (formerly known as Commission Junction). Each of these can direct you to the merchants best suited for you, allowing you to make the most money from your marketing affiliate program.

You'll want to pay close attention to how each one works and consider the impact it could have on your potential profits. For instance, Click bank lets you earn up to 75% of the product price and Pay Dotcom offers commissions up to 80%, but you may actually make more money off Amazon Affiliates even though they give you a lower percentage (6-15% depending on which program you choose) as they are one of the biggest online shopping retailers worldwide.

If you already have a successful blog or website that draws a lot of traffic, you may even get paid by a business for simply promoting their brand or name on your site, such as with Google Ad Sense. Options like this are often set up as pay-per-click, where you are reimbursed a certain rate for every person that clicks on the affiliate link that you have displayed somewhere on your site.

Step #5:

How to select an affiliate program to promote. I will review the process on Click Bank because it is the website I recommend you to start with. First and most important is the commission you will get for each sale.

Aim at 60%+ commissions for digital products. On average, most digital products on Click Bank sell between 35-85. Applying this rule you will be making at least 21$ per sale. If you promote physical products, don't stick with a specific percent but make sure you will earn at least 50$ per sale 6 since physical products tend to sell harder than digital ones.

Next make sure that the product has High Gravity. This means that a lot of people have made an affiliate sale in the past week, which basically means that the product is in high demand. However this will also mean that you have a lot of competition to sell the product. So my recommendation is to aim at products that have average gravity, but also have a great sales page. Make sure they have lengthy sales page and compare them with other competitive products, so you can see if they will covert well.

Step #6:

Create a link to the specific product(s) that you'd like to promote and earn a commission from and attach it to your site. Once you have selected an affiliate program you want to promote, you should get an affiliate link. It is important that you just paste it on your website, blog or channel.

If you place it on your website or blog, I recommend adding the link to the name of the program or something that represents it, instead of just pasting the link, which will be very unprofessional and also everyone will know that this is an affiliate link. If you are using YouTube to promote the product, you can use a link shortener like this one by Google "https://goo.gl." This way your links will look much more professional.

Step #7:

Market your link. Now that your site is set up and ready to earn you some money, you must market your affiliate products as if they were your very own. Get your readers and followers interested in the items, programs, or services you have chosen so that they are willing to click on them and most importantly buy them.

Not only you want to promote these things on your base site, but don't be afraid to post about them (with the links) in groups or forums that are relevant to your target market too. The more exposure you can get, the higher your chance of making sales—and money.

EARNING POTENTIAL

So, how much money can you make as an affiliate marketer? According to a poll conducted by Finch Sells, the majority of affiliates (just under 19 percent) earn $20,000 or less annually. Don't let that discourage you though. Almost six percent of the respondents reported that they earn over two million dollars a year by selling other people's products, services, and brands. That's worth it, right?

Therefore, it's largely up to you how far you will go and how much you stand to make with this particular online money making option. Obviously, the more traffic you can draw to your pages and the more time you put into promoting yourself and the affiliates that you've chosen to do business with, the more successful you will be.

If you want to increase your earning potential, it may benefit you to join an affiliate marketing forum like Digital Point, Warrior Forum, or a BestWeb. Forums such as these allow you to interact with other affiliate marketers who can provide you with the tips and tricks you need to help you succeed, thereby allowing you to earn a higher income at a faster rate than if you try to figure out affiliate marketing all on your own.

4 YOUTUBE

YouTube is the most popular video sharing website in the world, so I guess you are familiar with it to some extent. You can make money on it by creating your own channel and promoting either your own or other businesses' services and products, or you can participate in the YouTube Partner Program.

HOW TO GET STARTED

YouTube is much like any other social media site as far as set-up goes. But here are the steps you need to take to create a video channel worthy of hundreds, thousands, or even millions of viewers daily:

Step #1:

Create your YouTube channel. Google has easy to follow, in-depth instructions that will help make the process of creating your own YouTube channel fairly simple. But first, you need to decide whether you want to set it up in your own name or the name of your business (if you have one). Think of what you want as your brand and choose the one that makes the most sense for you.

Also, another important factor to consider when creating your YouTube account is that you want to select keywords that your target market will likely use when they search for the products and services that you're selling so that you're more likely to show up in their results list. For instance, if your videos are about personal development, some good keywords include: raising self-esteem, feeling better about yourself, how to be self-confident, and developing a self-empowering attitude.

Once you get the logistics out of the way, you need to create an attractive YouTube channel. To do this, be sure to pick the right theme and color scheme for your topic area, and be sure to upload a picture that is representative of you or your brand so that your viewers can start to connect with you.

You must also select a video for your featured video on your YouTube channel, so make sure it is one of your best. Keep in mind that this may be what gets your target market to sign up for your posts (or leave your channel), so it needs to be one that entices them to do what you'd like.

Fill in the title and description using content that represents what you have to offer in a fun and interesting way. Any fields that you don't fill in should be removed so they don't clutter up your page, but be sure to leave the comment option intact on as this encourages your followers to connect with you, thereby raising your interaction, and your sales!

Step #2:

Post videos. Once your YouTube channel is created, then

you are ready to post your videos to it. What types of videos do best? Well, it depends on what you're trying to accomplish with them. Generally, shorter, high quality videos seem to get the most views. Therefore, it may be worth it to invest in good equipment and engage the help of friends so that you're not trying to do everything solo.

On the other hand, if you're demonstrating something or making a how-to video, it may need to be longer in length in order to convey a complete message. You want to get all of the necessary information in without talking fast or skipping over things in an effort to reduce your time.

To decide which will work best for your needs, think of what your target market would like to see and do your videos with those thoughts in mind. If you don't know, ask them and let them tell you what to direct next!

Step #3:

Build your audience. As was mentioned in step one, selecting good keywords for your content helps drive traffic to your channel so keep that in mind when you're trying to target a select group of individuals. Use Google Keyword Planner to search for keywords based on your channel's niche. Make a list of the highest searched keywords. You should come up with about 20 here. List the keyword phrase along with the number of monthly searches. These are search keywords.

Next visit YouTube and make sure that you're logged out. We're going to be using the search function. Get the list that you just made and type the first three-four letters of the keyword phrase. YouTube will start listing suggestions as you type. This is no coincidence. These are keywords that other users are using to search for videos. You want to match these suggestions to the keywords in your list.

These are your target audience's keywords.

And just as you should regularly post with other forms of social media, the same applies with YouTube. This will get more and more people to subscribe to your channel since they know that you will be uploading content consistently, making it easier to create a following.

Step #4:

Cross-promote your videos. Share your videos on other forms of social media, such as Facebook and Twitter, to lead your followers and connections back to your YouTube site.

Encourage them to subscribe to your channel so they can easily see what you are going to do next. If you don't tell them to, they might not even think of it on their own. Get them excited about what you have to offer and make them want to be a part of it!

You can also start a website and/or blog and promote your videos there. I recommend that you use WordPress for the purpose, because it is free and very easy to set up. However I recommend that you invest 10$ in buying a domain name and also BUY a hosting for your website (you can use www.bsolve.in since they have really good prices). Free hosting is your worst enemy, never use it, because it will flood your website with random advertisement and it will look extremely unprofessional in the eyes of your audience.

Step #5:

Set your YouTube account up to monetize with ads. You can take this step either right when you are uploading your video or after it is already live (although the first option is recommended so that you don't miss out on any cash). Do this by checking the "Monetize with Ads" option which can be found on the upload screen or by going to your Video Manager and doing it there after the fact.

Once your account is ready to be monetized, you'll also want to go to the Google AdSense website and create an account there. In order to do this, you need to be 18 years of age and have either a PayPal account or a bank account to get paid, so keep these parameters in mind before wasting your time by finding out that you don't have what you need.

Some ads are Cost per Click (CPC), which means that your advertiser pays when their ad is clicked on. Other ads are Cost per View (CPV), which requires that your viewer watch at least half of their ad, or 30 seconds worth, whichever comes first. Pre-roll ads are the ones that play prior to your video, while ads can also appear at the bottom of your video screen (called in-search ads) or on the side of it (in-display ads).

Each one has their own advantages, so it is really up to you which ones you want to use. You may even decide to try a couple of them and see which ones work best for your viewers. Change them around and see if it makes a difference for your income.

Step #6:

Monetize your YouTube channel with affiliate marketing.

Remember how the section on affiliate marketing said that you can make money on any Internet site? Well, YouTube is one of them, allowing you to direct your target market to the products and services that you feel will benefit them most by putting links on your YouTube page, making you money by selling other people's goods.

Again, you want to choose affiliates that would appeal to your target audience. So, choose the products and services most appropriate for your consumer so that you can make the most money possible.

You can also sell your own products and services on YouTube, earning 100 percent of the income, which is always a good thing.

Step #7:

Check your stats and use the information wisely. YouTube provides you with analytics as to your video views so check them and see which ones are doing the best. Also, pay attention to which videos or topics aren't generating much buzz as that is equally as important to know.

The second part of this step involves using this information wisely. This means making changes to your strategy if something isn't working, but it also requires that you make more videos like the ones that are doing the best and capturing the most attention.

Step #8:

Optional: Apply for a YouTube partnership. This particular step is only available to you after your YouTube channel has met certain criteria.

Why apply for partnership? Because you have more content creation tools at your disposal and you can possibly win prizes based on the success of your channel. Either way, it is good for you.

EARNING POTENTIAL

It is important to realize that you don't make money on YouTube based on the number of followers you have, but on how many of them engage with your ads and affiliates. Although they are definitely related, they are still independent of each other, which mean that you need to get your followers involved. It's not enough to just have them watch your videos.

One way to do this is to talk about your affiliates, ads, and products in your video. Give a call to action that tells your viewer to click on the links. If you don't, you may be wasting a good opportunity to increase your income.

So, how much money can you realistically make with YouTube videos? According to an article written by Business Insider, you can earn six figures with the right content, just like Olga Kay does, however it's likely going to cost you.

On the other hand you have many examples of twenty YouTube millionaires like Vitalyzd TV who has almost 8 million subscribers and make a fortune from his videos.

So is it worth it? Only you know the answer to that. It's possible that you may decide that this option may be best as a side job or you can device do dive in and do your best to make your star shine on YouTube, just go for whichever option you feel right at the moment.

5 BLOGGING

A third way to make money online is by blogging. Blogging is defined as continuously writing about a situation, event, or other interest and posting it online for others to read. If you can create quite a following with your blog, you can also create a decent income.

INTRODUCTION TO ONLINE JOURNALING

Blogging and social networking are inextricably linked in the sense that both contain certain features and certain properties of one another. Both are aimed at creating a wide movement as far as multimedia interaction is concerned. Though it is true that blogs can be regulated and kept very private, the main purpose of them is to reach out to a number of people, to have a medium to voice your opinion.

Another similarity is that both these concepts have existed in cyber space for almost a decade now, but in the initial stages both were rather exclusive of one another. Only in the recent times have they been merged, and their similarity in motives truly recognized.

Blogging is essentially done to channel your thoughts out on to an online journal. You also want other people to read what you have written.

This way, you go about coming in touch with people from all over the world who you would not have otherwise known. Similar is the function of social networking. It is a hub where the young and the hearty flock. The chances of getting an audience at such a platform are high.

The origination of the term 'blog' is interesting. It was initially called a 'weblog' meaning a log or a diary or a journal that helps you to record your thoughts on a day to day basis. In that sense it was rather in its primitive stages and did not turn into an instrument for propaganda immediately. This term was later shortened to blog and this is when free blogging services like Blogger became extremely popular.

As mentioned earlier, blogging today is not restricted to only maintaining a journal. It has truly become a platform where various kinds of people from all walks of life, whether they have the same ideologies or not, conflate, and discuss the matters they think are important to them.

Blogging in the twenty first century has come to become an important tool for advertising for people who wish to market their products online, for politicians who wish to sell their ideologies, and reach out, to the masses.

Moreover, creating a blog and maintaining it does not require a fortune. Everybody now has a personal blog and it is all free of cost. Also, one does not need to be a computer engineer or a graphic or web designer in order to embellish their blog.

Unlike a website which operates on a different domain, and for which every single template and tab needs to be designed and created from the scratch, blog sites do not need such knowledge. The blogging service providers have their own inbuilt templates and fonts which have to be chosen by the bloggers as per their own tastes and preferences.

Blogging is an ideal way to make new friends and come in contact with more people than you can do in the actual word, from all quarters of the world. Such diverse people will obviously have differing viewpoints. Therefore, this gives scope for a good deal of discussion and debate with all points of view being taken on board.

Blogs can also be for the sole purpose of making new friends and socializing. That is why social networking sites have picked up the clue and in these times social networking and blogging has, to some extent, been combined, and almost become indistinguishable.

It would be interesting to note that the word 'blog' is both a noun and a verb. This leads us to the fact that blogging in some sense also helps get rid of hassles of publishing.

Though your work will not come out in print, you know that you can publish your work –your articles, pictures, videos, etc – yourself through you blog.

Therefore, it may be your own personal journal that you wish others to read or you works of art in terms of the stories or articles that you write, or the movies that you make. You can share almost any content with the world at large.

It must also be noted that just like you do not have to be a web designer to create your own blog, you need not be a professional writer, a film maker or a photographer to publish content on your blog. It is just a space for you to indulge in your own small artistic pursuits and share those moments with others. Blogging must therefore be exploited to its full potential.

HOW CAN BLOGGING BE PROFITABLE TO INDIVIDUAL?

Ranking of any website depends on a few factors. It would basically depend on the relevance of the article according to the key words used; the number of times that page has been linked and viewed, etc.

These are quite easy to follow, and if these factors are carefully noted and looked into, the rankings of your website can increase considerably.

The first step is to get your website linked through various other pages. The more the pages are that contain your links, the better ranking they will receive. The second aspect to be kept in mind is how often you update the content on your website.

Frequently edited and updated sites receive higher ranking in search engines than those that have not been looked at by the owners for ages. Always editing the content of your website as a whole may not be an option.

In this case what you can do is add a Blog to your website. A Blog will function as nothing but a forum for people to come and discuss the themes that concern your website too.

It will create a platform, as well as become a journal whereby you can also post updates about your operations and your website. The advantage is that the content on such Blogs will not be restricted only to text, but pictures and videos can be posted too.

The few easy steps as described below will take you through how to create your own blog and what are the things you must look out for:

☐

☐ Cost can never be a problem because free blogging services are quite popular all over the world. If you choose sites like Blogger or LiveJournal, you are sure to get exactly the kind of platform you are looking for. They are absolutely free.

☐ If you are not very comfortable with web designing techniques, you need not worry. Creating your blog is not as complicated as designing template for a website. These blogging services provide a wide range of templates from which you can choose the one most suited to your tastes.

☐ You must also use your discretion while blogging. Especially if you are incorporating your blog within your website, or creating a blog to increase awareness of your product, you need to keep in mind that this is an open forum which is read by all. You do not want to say anything that may end up angering your clients. Politics and religion are the two most controversial themes, and therefore anything about those must be carefully blogged about.

☐ Anything that is particularly reader friendly and does not anger too many people is considered 'safe'. If your aim is indeed to increase the ranking of your site, you will have to make sure many people read it. You can do this by making your content user friendly.

☐ Also keep an eye on what other people write or say on their blogs. This can give you a general idea of what kind of responses those articles receive, and you can get valuable tips from them.

Blogging has come to be considered a highly effective marketing tool. You can easily create awareness of your product and get clients and customers to interact with each other. And not only customers, also those who are relatively new to your product get a platform to ask questions and clear their air about your product.

Moreover, it also increases your website rankings can increase because the blog is constantly being updates, commented on, and discussions are always going on. Because of its sheer activity, the rankings improve, creating more awareness of the product.

The following are the pointers based on which you can blog about your product:
☐

☐ Never make the blog post too long uselessly. It must be well written. Long posts tend to get dreary and they are not 'catchy' enough for people to sit and go through them.

☐ Update regularly. Since you don't need to write long posts, that is not much effort. Ideally, blog 3-7 times a week.☐

☐ Be entertaining where required, everyone can do with some light hearted humor, without being derogatory.

☐ You need not stick only to text. Video and photo blogging are fats catching on and are interesting ways to share your thoughts, and make your videos and photographs well known.

☐ Be yourself. Do not to ape, imitate or copy someone else's content.

HOW TO GET STARTED

To create a blog that draws major attention and begin to draw money from it, here's what you need to do:

Step #1:

Decide what you want your blog to be about. What topic or topics interest you most? Are you a car geek who knows everything and anything about the cars and trucks on the road today, or do you have an insatiable appetite for cooking and want to share your passion with others who feel the same?

Some of the most profitable niches and blog ideas are tech review blogs, beauty and fashion, health and nutrition, how to make money, or even teaching people how to blog! However, it is very important to only blog about things that you are genuinely interested in. Otherwise, you won't be able to engage other people in the topic if you have no interest in it yourself.

Once you have a list of options, pick a topic and tailor it down as specifically as you can to better resonate with your target market. For instance, if you enjoy cooking, what style speaks to you most? Are you a farm-to-table chef or do you like making traditional foods with a modern flair? The more specific you can make your topic, the easier it will be to reach the people you intend to reach.

To look for inspiration with this, check out related blogs that others are writing. This may help you come up with ideas for your own, in addition to helping you see what parts of their blog you like, and which ones you don't, making your blog easier for you to create, which is the next step.

Step #2:

Create your blog. If you already have a blog in place, you are one step ahead of the game. If not, then you need to create one. You can do this by putting a blog page on your own website, or by joining a pre-existing blog platform, such as WordPress, that has easy-to-use themes that make setting up your blog a cinch.

Your number one priority is to come up with a domain name that suits you and is easy for your followers to remember and recognize. Something short and catchy will often do the trick, like 3 Fat Chicks who offer weight loss support or Dumb Little Man who provides tips about life. Also, don't try get too close to a well-known trademarked name in an attempt to get more followers or you could run into problems.

If you are setting up your blog on a self-hosting website such as Besolve, Hostgator, Bluehost, or Dreamhost, all of which have packages for less than $1 per month, remember that .com's often work the best as that is what most people are used to. At this point, .net is becoming more universal as well, so that is an option you may want to consider.

You also want to create a page that is pleasing to your target market and consistent with your brand. Choose colors and graphics that are representative of your style and topic, making it easy for your potential client base to tell who and what you are about at a glance.

Step #3:

Start posting. The key to effective blogging is to create articles that your target market would want to read that contain keywords so you are easier to find. This involves creating a title that draws them in and writing a blog that engages interests, entertains, and benefits them in some way, while still making sure that each part of your blog has the keywords where they need to be. Also always format your articles to look appealing and to be easier to read.

You can either write these on your own or hire a ghostwriter to write them for you. If you choose a ghostwriter, one great platform to hire from is Elance. Each freelance writer is rated based on their past performance with previous clients, allowing you to pick the one that is best for you after reviewing their profile and job proposal on your specific project.

Don't be afraid to post videos or pictures on your blog either. People resonate with different types of material, so mix your blog up to suit most every type of reader or viewer and you'll have a larger impact, as well as a larger following.

One very important thing to remember is to post regularly. Get your readers used to seeing your name so they feel like you're a trusted friend and make them look forward to your posts, as if you are a part of their everyday life.

Some people choose to post on a specific schedule, like every Saturday morning at 8:00 AM. However, others post randomly and only when they have something to say. Find what works best for you and stick to it. I recommend that in the beginning you post as much as possible, without sacrificing quality of course. Aim at 2-3 times a week in order to build a larger following on your blog.

Step #4:

Build your following by promoting your blog. Once you have some posts on your blog, now is a good time to promote it to build your following. First and foremost, you want to add the right keywords to your blog and the posts it contains so that your target market can easily find you when they do a search.

Second, you want to encourage them to follow your blog by offering a free download upon signing up, building your followers quicker and more effectively. Put a "Subscribe" button on it so that they can easily sign up to receive your posts as you make them (I recommend using AWeber.com or mailchimp.com for this purpose). Ask them to share them with their family and friends, who can then subscribe as well.

Step #5:

Monetise your blog. Implementing what you've already learned about making money online in Chapter 1, your blog is a great place for affiliate marketing and CPC (Cost Per Click) ad networks like Google AdSense. Both of these options can draw in some good money if you have a huge following on your blog.

CPM ad networks will also pay you for reaching your viewers. The rate is measured per 1,000, so the more followers you have, the more money you stand to make. Some options, if this is a route you choose to take, are AdClickMedia, Twelvefold Media, and SiteScout.

Additionally, you can sell your own products and services on your blog too and monetize it that way. If you're a freelance writer, for instance, you can offer your followers content packages for their business (such as for their web page, emails, or their blog), or if you are a motivational speaker, you 15 can offer to talk to organizations and groups to inspire them to reach higher levels and achieve higher goals.

You could also create your own e-book (which we'll go over in this book) and sell it on your blog for some residual income that could really add up over time. Be creative with monetizing your blog and think of the endless possibilities when it comes to making money on it.

Step #6:

Promote your blog. Promote your blog on other platforms (such as your web page, social media accounts like Facebook and Twitter, YouTube, etc.) to draw others to it. Follow and post on other people's blogs, inspiring their curiosity to go to your blog and check out what it is about.

Since you already have content on your blog posting the same content as a video on YouTube, is an easy way to reach more people and invite them to your blog, and also a lot of people these days prefer to watch videos, rather than reading articles.

Another option is to allow guest posting on your blog, making others to want to be a part of it. This also helps them share your blog as well, as it benefits them to get their name out while getting yours out at the same time.

Join LinkedIn groups about and for bloggers and any other blogging groups you can find. When people ask questions within these groups about your topic, write a blog about it and refer them to it. It's a great way to establish you as an expert in the field, making them more likely to buy the products and services you recommend.

EARNING POTENTIAL

Here's the big question: How much can you earn by blogging? Well, depending on how big you grow your blog and how you choose to monetize it, you can make over $2 million per month, like the Huffington Post whose main income is in pay per click ads. Or you could make a lot less, such as Expert Photography who draws in roughly $5,000 per month via affiliate sales.

Some blogs don't make anything because they don't entice their reader to want to take action. Remember that while you're having fun with your blog, you're not going to make any money with it if you don't ask your readers to buy your products, purchase your affiliate's products, or click on the ads.

Find what works best for you and what connects most with your target market and you're on your way to creating a blog that brings in more in a month than some people make in a year. Who knows? Your blog may just be the next one to go viral, earning you a great annual income that will give you a nice, comfy life, long into retirement.

GETTING CONTSTANT TRAFFIC TO YOUR BLOG

Blogging has truly revolutionized the way one experiences the digital age. There is, it seems, no limit to what one can do with the help of blogs. Even the smallest aspect of your daily personal life like recording journal entries has been given an entirely new dimension.

Going on from there, there is a lot of scope of picking up interesting debates and discussions through blogs. You can even start some of these discussions yourself.

Moreover, there is nothing as interesting and attractive than that fact that you can even earn some money while blogging.

This is, by far, the most path breaking innovation that has entered the blog sphere. The requirements for this are very low. You need not be a scientist who posts revolutionary details about his latest experiment.

If you blog well, that is to say, if you blog well enough for people to come read it, you earn good chances of making quick money, by just going about your daily activity of posting blogs!

Here are some of the things you can do to make sure that your blogging activities get rewarded by more than just comments and praises:

You could get yourself registered with a search engine. But keep in mind that you must do it only if you are confident enough that your blog gets good traffic. That way, the higher the ranking your blog achieves, the more you get paid.

While writing your blogs you also need to keep in mind a few things. This is not only to ensure that you get a steady traffic, but also for the fact that your blog readership can increase so that the ranking of your blog with search engines go higher.

Here are a few tips that should see you through this:

    Reader Friendly Content: At all costs keep your content – articles, poems, photographs, videos –

reader friendly, that is to say, it should keep more and more readers interested. Your reader must be at the center of you post in a way that your reader must feel that he is gaining something out of reading your post.

This is the basic rule in marketing.

Worthwhile: Never let the reader feel that he has been tricked into reading your post or clicking on your blog link. You are thwarting all your long term chances of that reader coming back to your blog, in which case your blog rankings over the long term are in a dicey position.

Check for errors: Making grammatical and spelling errors can be a major put off for many readers. They may not visit your blog again simply because the errors that you make are too high. Always proof read your blog. A small typo here and there can be understood, but make sure you don't make any major errors.

KISS: Or, Keep It Short and Simple. This is the thumb rule you must follow at all point. Long winding posts tend to get boring. And it may contain nothing that is interesting to the reader. Also no one has the time enough for your blog, no matter how well you write. In fact, your blog will be much more appreciated if you put your thoughts simply and shortly.

Interesting: Make sure that you hold your reader's attention by making your posts snazzy. They must not be written in a tone that is tiring to read. Write short sentences and keep then crisp and precise. Always hit the point immediately in the course of your article.

Link: Keep linking the blogs you read to yours in order to build a network those people will be in turn encouraged to link you. Remember, linking increases rankings.

Keywords: Using the keywords of your posts frequently increases the search ability of that particular article of yours which in turn leads more people to visit your blog.

Clear Thoughts: Make sure you put your thought clearly before the readers so that it does not become tedious for them to read.

Colloquialism: You can write in a friendly tone. Avoid using too many slang
words, but otherwise, if your post demands it, you can be colloquial.

Post Title: A catchy post title or headline is half your business solved. It can glue a reader to your post almost immediately. However, do not put misleading post titles, or you will lose creditability.

So, be consistent with your blog content and watch traffic flowing in to your blog!

6 GOOGLE ADSENSE A-TO-Z

For the last couple of years, Google AdSense has dominated forums, discussions and newsletters all over the Internet. Already, there are tales of fabulous riches to be made and millions made by those who are just working from home. It seems that Google AdSense have already dominated the internet marketing business and is now considered the easiest way to making money online.

The key to success with AdSense is the placing of ads on pages that are receiving high traffic for high demand keywords. The higher the cost-per-click to the advertiser, the more you will receive per click from your site. Obviously, it does not pay to target low cost-per-click keywords and place them on pages that do not receive hits.

With all the people getting online and clicking away everyday, it is no wonder why Google AdSense has become an instant hit.

For some who are just new to this market, it would be a blow to their pride knowing that their homepage is buried somewhere in the little ads promoting other people's services. But then, when they get the idea that they are actually earning more money that way, all doubts and skepticism is laid to rest.

There are two major, and clever, factors that some successful webmaster and publishers are learning to blend together in order to make money easier using AdSense.

> 1. Targeting high traffic pages on your website. If you check on your logs, you will discover that many of your visitors are taking advantage of the free affiliate marketing

resources and ebooks that you are offering on your site. In simple words, your ads are working effectively and are generating more clicks. It also means more money for you.

2. Placing AdSense links on pages that are producing little, or better yet, no profit. By placing AdSense on a free resources page, you will reduce the amount of potential customers being lost to other sites. Tricky, but effective nonetheless.

When learned to work effectively, these two factors are actually a good source of producing a minimal amount of revenue from a high traffic page. Many people are using this strategy to pick up some extra and cash with AdSense. This is also especially rewarding to informational sites that focus their efforts on delivering powerful affiliate link free content to their visitors. Now they can gain a monetary return on their services.

With the many techniques that people are now learning on how to make the easiest money by their AdSense, it is not surprising that Google is trying everything to update and polish their AdSense in order to maintain their good image.

The possibility of adding is 2nd tier in AdSense is not impossible. With all the people spending more time in their AdSense now and still more getting into this line of marketing, there is no doubt about the many new improvements yet to be made. Imagine the smiles on the faces of the webmasters and publishers all around the world if ever they sign up for sub-affiliates and double or even triple the amount that they are already earning.

The one particularly handy money-making feature that is available with AdSense now is the ability to filter out up to 200 urls. These gives webmasters the option to block out low value offers from their pages as well as competitors to their websites. Talk about taking only those that are advantageous and discarding the ones that seem "useless".

With Google AdSense, the possibilities are limitless. Yet there is also the possibility of someone taking advantage of the easy money process that this internet marketing is doing.

If you think more about it, these negative factors may force Google to break down and thrash AdSense in the process.

If that happens, people would have to go back to the old ways of internet marketing that does not make money online as easy as AdSense.

For now, however, Google AdSense is here to stay. As long as there are people wanting to earn some easy cash online just using their talents, the future ahead is looking good. Besides with all the strict guidelines that Google is enforcing over AdSense, it will take a while for the AdSense privileges to be spammed and even terminated.

3 REASONS WHY ADSENSE IS ESSENTIAL

To know why AdSense is essential for your content sites is to know first how this works.

The concept is really simple, if you think about it. The publisher or the webmaster inserts a java script into a certain website. Each time the page is accessed, the java script will pull advertisements from the AdSense program.

The ads that are targeted should therefore be related to the content that is contained on the web page serving the ad. If a visitor clicks on an advertisement, the webmaster serving the ad earns a portion of the money that the advertiser is paying the search engine for the click.

The search engine is the one handling all the tracking and payments, providing an easy way for webmasters to display content-sensitive and targeted ads without having the hassle to solicit advertisers, collect funds, monitor the clicks and statistics which could be a time-consuming task in itself.

It seems that there is never a shortage of advertisers in the program from which the search engine pulls the AdSense ads. Also webmasters are less concerned by the lack of information search engines are providing and are more focused in making cash from these search engines.

The first reason why AdSense is essential for content sites is because it already has come a long way in understanding the needs of publishers and webmasters.

Together with its continuous progression is the appearance of more advanced system that allows full ad customization. Webmasters are given the chance to choose from many different types of text ad formats to better complement their website and fit their webpage layout.

The different formatting enables the site owners the possibility of more click through from visitors who may or may not be aware of what they are clicking on. It can also appeal to the people visiting thus make them take that next step of looking up what it is all about. This way the people behind the AdSense will get their content read and making profit in the process.

The second reason is the ability of the AdSense publishers to track not only how their sites are progressing but also the earnings based on the webmaster-defined channels. The recent improvements in the search engines gives webmasters the capability to monitor how their ads are performing using customizable reports that has the capacity to detail page impressions, clicks and click-through rates.

Webmasters and publishers can now track specific ad formats, colors and pages within a website. Trends are also easily spotted.

With the real-time reporting at hand, the effectiveness of the changes made will be assessed quickly. There would be time to sort out the contents that people are making the most clicks on. The ever-changing demands would be met while generating cash for the webmasters and publishers.

The more flexible tools are also allowing webmasters to group web pages by URL, domain, ad type or category, which will provide them some accurate insight on which pages, ads and domains are performing best.

The last and final reason is that the advertisers have realized the benefits associated having their ads served on targeted websites. Thus increasing the possibility that a prospective web surfer will have an interest in their product and services. All because of the content and its constant maintenance.

As opposed to those who are no using AdSense in their sites, they are given the option of having other people do their content for them, giving them the benefit of having successful and money-generating websites.

AdSense is all about targeted content, the more targeted your content is, the more target the search engines' ads will be. There are some web masters and publishers who are focused more on their site contents and how best to maintain them rather than the cash that the ads will generate for them. This is the part where the effectiveness is working its best.

There was a time when people were not yet aware of the money to be achieved from advertisements. The cash generated only came into existence when the webmasters and publishers realized how they can make AdSense be that generator. In those days, the content were the most important factors that is taken quite seriously. It still is. With the allure of money, of course.

HOW TO START MAKING MONEY WITH ADSENSE

AdSense is considered as one of the most powerful tool in a website publisher's arsenal. It enables a person to monetize their sites easily. If used properly, it can generate a very large and healthy income for them. However if you are not using them rightly and just maximizing the income you squeeze from it, you are actually leaving a lot of money on the table. Something all people hate doing.

How you can start earning money with AdSense can be done easily and quickly. You will be amazed at the results you will be getting in such a short period of time.

Start by writing some quality content articles which are also keyword incorporated. There are a lot of people given the gift of being good with words. Writing comes easy for them. Why not make it work in such a way that you will be earning some extra cash in the process.

There are actually three steps to put into mind before you begin writing your ads and having an effective AdSense.

Keyword search. Find some popular subjects, keywords or phrase. Select the ones which you think has more people clicking through. This is actually a keyword selector and suggestion tool that some sites are offering to those who are just their AdSense business.

Writing articles. Start writing original content with keywords from the topics that you have achieved in your search. Take note that search engines are taking pride in the quality of their articles and what you will be writing should keep up with their demands.

Quality content site. Build a quality content site incorporated with AdSense ads that is targeting the subject and keywords of your articles and websites. This is where all that you've done initially will go to and this is also where they will prove their worth to you.

The proper positioning of your ads should be done with care. Try to position your ads where surfers are most likely to click on them. According to research, the one place that surfers look first when they visit a certain site is the top left. The reason behind this is not known. Maybe it is because some of the most useful search engine results are at the top of all other rankings. So visitors tend to look in that same place when browsing through other sites.

Some of those who are just starting at this business may think they are doing pretty well already and thinking that their click through rates and CPM figures are quite healthy. However, there are more techniques and styles to generate more clicks to double your earnings. By knowing these techniques and working them to your advantage, you will realize that you will be getting three times more than other people who have been previously doing what they are doing.

Finally, AdSense has some excellent tracking statistics that allows webmasters and publishers to track their results across a number of site on a site by site, page by page, or any other basis you wanted. You should be aware of this capability and make the most of it because it is one powerful tool that will help you find out which ads are performing best. This way, you can fine tune your AdSense ads and focus more on the ones being visited the most rather than those who are being ignored.

Another thing you should know. Banners and skyscrapers are dead. Ask the experts. So better forget about banners and skyscrapers. Surfers universally ignore these kinds of ad formats. The reason behind this is that they are recognized as an advert and advert are rarely of any interest that's why people ignore them.

To really start making money with AdSense, you should have a definite focus on what you wanted to achieve and how you will go about achieving them. As with any other kind of business ventures, time is needed coupled with patience.

Do not just ignore your site and your AdSense once you have finished accomplishing them. Spare some time, even an hour, making adjustments to the AdSense ads on your sites to quickly trigger your AdSense income.

Give it a try and you would not regret having gotten into AdSense in the first place.

5 WAYS TO IMPROVE YOUR ADSENSE EARNINGS

If webmasters want to monetize their websites, the great way to do it is through AdSense. There are lots of webmasters struggling hard to earn some good money a day through their sites. But then some of the "geniuses" of them are enjoying hundreds of dollars a day from AdSense ads on their websites. What makes these webmasters different from the other kind is that they are different and they think out of the box.

The ones who have been there and done it have quite some useful tips to help those who would want to venture into this field. Some of these tips have boosted quite a lot of earnings in the past and is continuously doing so.

Here are 5 proven ways on how best to improve your AdSense earnings.

1. Concentrating on one format of AdSense ad. The one format that worked well for the majority is the Large Rectangle (336X280). This same format have the tendency to result in higher CTR, or the click-through rates. Why choose this format out of the many you can use? Basically because the ads will look like normal web links, and people, being used to clicking on them, click these types of links. They may or may not know they are clicking on your AdSense but as long as there are clicks, then it will all be for your advantage.

2. Create a custom palette for your ads. Choose a color that will go well with the background of your site. If your site has a white background, try to use white as the color of your ad border and background. The idea to patterning the colors is to make the AdSense look like it is part of the web pages. Again, this will result to more clicks from people visiting your site.

3. Remove the AdSense from the bottom pages of your site and put them at the top. Do not try to hide your AdSense. Put them in the place where people can see them quickly. You will be amazed how the difference between AdSense locations can make when you see your earnings.

4. Maintain links to relevant websites. If you think some sites are better off than the others, put your ads there and try to maintaining and managing them. If there is already lots of AdSense put into that certain site, put yours on top of all of them. That way visitor will see your ads first upon browsing into that site.

5. Try to automate the insertion of your AdSense code into the webpages using SSI (or server side included). Ask your web administrator if your server supports SSI or not. How do you do it? Just save your AdSense code in a text file, save it as "adsense text", and upload it to the root directory of the web server. Then using SSI, call the code on other pages. This tip is a time saver especially for those who are using automatic page generators to generate pages on their website.

These are some of the tips that have worked well for some who want to generate hundreds and even thousands on their websites. It is important to know though that ads are displayed because it fits the interest of the people viewing them. So focusing on a specific topic should be your primary purpose because the displays will be especially targeted on a topic that persons will be viewing already.

Note also that there are many other AdSense sharing the same topic as you. It is best to think of making a good ad that will be somewhat different and unique than the ones already done. Every clickthrough that visitors make is a point for you so make every click count by making your AdSense something that people will definitely click on.

Tips given by those who have boosted their earnings are just guidelines they want to share with others. If they have somehow worked wonders to some, maybe it can work wonders for you too. Try them out into your ads and see the result it will bring.

If others have done it, there is nothing wrong trying it out for yourself.

MONETISING YOUR WEBSITE WITH ADSENSE

Many are now realising that good money is made from this source of revenue. Try the simple mathematical computation of multiplying those clicks for every page on your website and you get a summation of earnings equivalent to a monthly residual income with that little effort you have made.

Google AdSense is a fast and easy way for website publishers of all sizes to display relevant and text-based Google ads on their website's content pages and earn money in the process. The ads displayed are related to what your users are looking for on your site. This is the main reason why you both can monetize and enhance your content pages using AdSense.

How much you will be earning will depend on how much the advertisers are willing to pay. It will depend also on the keywords required. If the keywords the advertiser have chosen are in high demand, you could receive more dollars per click. On the other hand, low demand keywords will earn you just a few cents per click.

How can you start making profits out of your website using AdSense?

1. Sign up for an AdSense account. It will only take a few minutes of your time.

2. When the site is accepted, you will be receiving a clip code to include in your web pages. You can insert this code on as many pages or web sites that you want. The AdWords will start appearing immediately after.

3. You will be earning a few cents or some dollars per click when someone starts clicking on the AdWords displayed on any of your web pages. Trying to earn false revenues by repetitively clicking on your own ads is a no-no. This will result in a penalty or the possibility of your site being eliminated. The money you have already earned may be lost because of this.

4. View your statistics. AdSense earnings can be checked anytime by logging into your web site account.

Once you got your account working, you may still want to pattern them to the many sites that are earning more money than you are. It is important to note that there are factors affecting how your website will perform and the amount of money it will give you.

It is a common practice that when a site earning money, the tendency is for the owner to want to make more out of what they are getting already. It usually takes some time combined with trial and error to attain what you want for your AdSense contents.

Time and some important factors that you can practice and use.

How do you increase your AdSense earnings?

1. Choose one topic per page. It is best to write a content for your page with just a few targeted phrases. The search engine will then serve ads that are more relevant which will then result in higher clickthoughs.

2. Using white space around your ad. This can make your ad stand out from the rest of your page so visitors can spot them easily. There are also other choices of colors you can use, provided by search engines, which can harmonize the color of your ad with the web page color.

3. Test your ad placement. It is recommended to use the vertical format that runs down the side of the web page to get more positive results. You can also try both horizontal and vertical formats for a certain period of time to see which one will give you better results.

4. More content-based pages. Widen the theme of your website by creating pages that focus more on your keyword phrases. This will optimize the pages for the search engines. It can not only attract traffic but also make them more relevant for the AdWords to be displayed.

5. Site Build It. This is the perfect tool to be used for creating lots of AdSense revenues. Site Build It has all the tools necessary to quickly achieve a keyword-rich site that can rank high in the search engines. This will also produce a flow of traffic to your site of highly targeted visitors.

Most webmasters know that AdSense generates a sizeable source of additional advertising income. That is why most of them use it to go after high paying keywords.

They have with them the lists that tells what the keywords are and have already used various methods of identifying them. And yet, after putting up these supposed-to-be high paying keywords into their pages, the money they expected to come rolling in is not really coming in.

WHAT IS IT THAT THEY ARE DOING WRONG?

Having the pages is with the proper keywords is one thing. But driving visitors to those pages is another matter and often the factor that is lacking.

The thing is, to get visitors to your high paying keyword pages, you need to optimize your site navigation.

Stop for a moment and think about how visitors are using your website. After a visitor has landed on a certain page, they have the tendency to click on another page that sounds interesting. They get there because of the other links that appears on a page that they initially landed on. This is site navigation. It is all about enabling visitors to move about your site. And one way of maximizing your AdSense earnings.

A typical website have menu links on each page. The

wording on these links is what grabs a visitor's attention and gets them to click on one of the links that will take them to another page of that website. Links that have "free" or "download" are oftentimes good attention-grabbers.

This navigation logic can also be applied to driving traffic to your high paying pages. There are some websites that are getting a lot of traffic from search engines, but have low earnings. The trick is to try and use come cleverly labeled links to get the visitors off that pages and navigate them to the higher earning ones. This is one great way of turning real cheap clicks to real dollars.

Before you begin testing if this same style will work for you and you website, you need to have two things. Something to track and compare and some high earning pages you want to funnel your site traffic to. An option is to select a few of your frequently visited pages. This is ensuring fast result to come by.

Now, the next thing to do is think of ways to get visitors viewing a particular page to try and click on the link that will take them to your high earning pages. Come up with a catchy description for that link. Come up with a catchy and unique description for the link. Think of something that people do not get to see everyday. That will trigger their curiosity enough to try and see what that was all about.

You can also use graphics to grab your readers' attention. There is no limitation to what you can do to make your link noticeable. If you are after the success of your site, you will do everything it takes just to achieve that goal. Just be creative. As far as many AdSense advertisers are concerned, there are no written and unwritten laws to follow regarding what they write. Just as long as you do not overstep the guidelines of the search engines, then go for it.

Also remember that it is all about location, location and location. Once the perfect attention grabbing description has been achieved, you have to identify the perfect spot on your page to position that descriptive link to your high paying page.

There is nothing wrong with visiting other websites to see how they are going about maximizing their site navigation. "Hot pages" or "Most read" lists are very common and overly used already. Get to know the ones that many websites are using and do not try to imitate them.

Another way of doing it is to try and use different texts on different pages. That way you will see the ones that work and what does not. Try to mix things around also. Put links on top and sometimes on the bottom too. This is how you go about testing which ones get more clicks and which ones are being ignored.

Let the testing begin. Testing and tracking until you find the site navigation style that works best for you site.

INCREASE YOUR ADSENSE CASH

AdSense is really making a huge impact on the affiliate marketing industry nowadays. Because of this, weak affiliate merchants have the tendency to die faster than ever and ad networks will be going to lose their customers quickly.

If you are in a losing rather than winning in the affiliate program you are currently into, maybe it is about time to consider going into the AdSense marketing and start earning some real cash.

Google is readily providing well written and highly relevant ads that are closely chosen to match the content on your pages. You do not have to look for them yourselves as the search engine will be the doing the searching for you from other people's source.

You do not have to spend time in choosing different kind of ads for different pages. And no codes to mess around for different affiliate programs.

You will be able to concentrate on providing good and quality content, as the search engines will be the ones finding the best ads in which to put your pages on.

You are still allowed to add AdSense ads even if you already have affiliate links on your site. It is prohibited, however, to imitate the look and feel of the Google ads for your affiliate links.

You can filter up to 200 URLs. That gives you a chance to block ads for the sites that do not meet your guidelines. You can also block competitors. Though it is unavoidable that AdSense may be competing for some space on web sites that all other revenues are sharing.

Owners of small sites are allowed to plug a bit of a code into their sites and instantly have relevant text ads that appeal to your visitors appear instantly into your pages. If you own many sites, you only need to apply once. It makes up for having to apply to many affiliate programs.

The only way to know how much you are already earning is to try and see. If you want out, all you have to do is remove the code from your site.

The payment rates can vary extremely. The payment you will be receiving per click depends on how much advertisers are paying per click to advertise with the use of the AdWords. Advertisers can pay as little as 5 cents and as high as $10-12, sometimes even more than that too. You are earning a share of that money generated.

If your results remain stagnant, it can help if you try and build simple and uncluttered pages so that the ads can catch the visitor's eyes more. It sometimes pay to differ from the usual things that people are doing already. It is also a refreshing sight for your visitor once they see something different for a change.

Publishers also have the option of choosing to have their ads displayed only on a certain site or sites. It is also allowed to have them displayed on a large network of sites. The choice would be depending on what you think will work best for your advantage.

To get an idea if some AdSense ads you see on the search engines has your pages, try to find web pages that have similar material to the content you are planning to create and look up their AdSense ads.

It is important to note that you cannot choose certain topics only. If you do this, search engines will not place AdSense ads on your site and you will be missing out a great opportunity in making hundreds and even thousands of dollars cash.

It is still wise to look at other people's information and format your AdSense there. Just think about it as doing yourself a favor by not having to work too hard to know what content to have.

With all the information that people need in your hands already, all you have to do is turn them as your profits. It all boils down to a gain and gain situation both for the content site owners and the webmasters or publishers.

Make other people's matter your own and starting earning some extra cash.

AVOID GETTING YOUR ACCOUNT TERMINATED

Google, being the undisputable leader in search engines from then until now, is placing a high importance on the quality and relevancy of its search engines.

Most especially now that the company is public property. In order to keep the shareholders and users of its engines happy, the quality of the returned results are given extreme importance.

For this same reason, doing the wrong things in the AdSense and other forms of advertisements, whether intentionally or unintentionally, will result in a severe penalty, may get you banned and even have your account terminated. Nothing like a good action taken to keep wrongdoers from doing the same things over again.

So for those who are thinking of getting a career in AdSense, do not just think of the strategies you will be using to generate more earnings. Consider some things first before you actually get involved.

Hidden texts. Filling your advertisement page with texts to small to read, has the same color as the background and using CSS for the sole purpose of loading them with rich keywords content and copy will earn you a penalty award that is given to those who are hiding links.

Page cloaking. There is a common practice of using browser or bot sniffers to serve the bots of a different page other than the page your visitors will see. Loading a page with a bot that a human user will never see is a definite no-no. This is tricking them to click on something that you want but they may not want to go to.

Multiple submissions. Submitting multiple copies of your domain and pages is another thing to stay away from. For example, trying to submit a URL of an AdSense as two separate URL's is the same as inviting trouble and even termination.

Likewise, this is a reason to avoid auto submitters for those who are receiving submissions. Better check first if your domain is submitted already in certain search engine before you try to submit to it again. If you see it there, then move on. No point contemplating whether to try and submit there again.

Link farms. Be wary of who and what are you linking your AdSense to. The search engines know that you cannot control your links in. But you can certainly control what you link to. Link farming has always been a rotten apple in the eyes of search engines, especially Google. That is reason enough to try and avoid them. Having a link higher than 100 on a single page will classify you as a link farm so try and not to make them higher than that.

Page rank for sale. If you have been online for quite some time, you will notice that there are some sites selling their PR links or trading them with other sites. If you are doing this, expect a ban anytime in the future. It is okay to sell ads or gain the link. But doing it on direct advertisement of your page rank is a way to get on search engines bad side.

Doorways. This is similar to cloaking pages. The common practice of a page loaded with choice keyword ads aimed at redirecting visitors to another "user-friendly" page is a big issue among search engines. There are many SEO firms offering this kind of services. Now that you know what they actually are, try to avoid them at all costs.

Multiple domains having the same content. In case you are not aware of it, search engines look at domains IP's, registry dates and many others. Having multiple domains having the same exact content is not something you can hide from them. The same goes with content multiplied many times on separate pages, sub domains and forwarding multiple domains to the same content.

Many of the above techniques apply to most search engines and is not entirely for Google only. By having a mindset that you are building your AdSense together with your pages for the human users and not for bots, you can be assured of the great things for your ads and sites.

Not to mention avoiding the wrath of the search engines and getting your AdSense and site account terminated altogether.

7 FREELANCER

Fiverr/Freelancer is a website that allows you to sell your talent or talents for an income. For instance, are you a creative writer, SEO guru, design artist, website creator, or do you have talent as a voice-over artist? Then you can make money as a seller on Fiverr by providing your unique and talent-driven services to people and businesses whoever needs them.

HOW TO GET STARTED

To make money on Fiverr/Freelancer, just take these steps:

Step #1: Decide what you want to sell.

What products or services can you offer others relatively quickly and for a low starting amount (think $5 per gig)? Ideally, you want to come up with something unique so that you have less competition, but any skill that you have can easily be sold on Fiverr as there are lots of buyers available.

Step #2: Sign up for an account.

You can create a Fiverr account using your email address, Google+ account or Facebook to sign in. You just have to confirm it and then you are good to go.

Step #3: Set up your profile.

Once your account is created, you want to set up your profile, which means uploading a picture and telling Fiverr a little bit about who you are.

The consistent theme across this platform seems to be that less is better. So, you're going to want to be as clear and concise as you can in order to fit all of your content in. Be straight and to the point or you're going to be cut short. Also make sure that you use a professional looking photo for your profile picture (or your logo), you don't want to scare away potential buyers.

Step #4: Verify your idea.

But before you start creating your first gig, make sure that your idea is worthwhile. Go on fiverr and search for similar gigs. Make sure that there is a demand for similar services like yours.

Type your keywords and see if you can find at least 3 gigs that have more than 500 reviews and more than 10 orders in queue. If you find them, then good, this means that your idea is in high demand and you can make real money with it. Now let's proceed with creating your gig.

Step #5: Create a gig.

Click on "Start Selling" under your profile and create a gig, which is another name for the service or product you want to sell. We will break this step into smaller steps that need to be taken in order to build a bestselling gig.

So let's start with your gig title. You only have 80 characters for your gig title, so use them wisely. Fiverr even tells you that short titles sell more, so heed their advice, also it is very important that your title clearly describes what you offer; don't use confusing titles, because this will bring you a lot of angry buyers.

Next you want to have a very appealing and competitive

gig samples. Again make sure to take a look around Fiverr in order to see how people represent their gigs. Use this for inspiration and also for a reference how good your gig should look. If you can make it look better and more appealing than the other gigs that are already available, then great. If you are not a graphic designer consider hiring one from fiverr who can create you cool images to represent your gig.

After you are done with your samples you should continue with the gig description. Make sure that you use the formatting options that fiverr offers, so it can be easy to read and highlight all the key points. Explain your service in detail, what you offer for 5$ and what you offer as an extra. Look at your description as a contract with the client that defines your service.

Next it is recommended that you upload a video. Gigs that have a video tend to gain popularity more easily, because they get a better placement in the search results when they are published. You can simply record yourself explaining your service, also don't forget to mention the phrase "this gig is exclusively on fiverr.com", and make sure that your video looks professional and you don't have your bed in the background or something embarrassing.

Step #6: Promote your gig.

Fiverr makes this step super easy as well as once you have all of the information they are requesting, you can publish your gig via social media buttons before even leaving the page. They have one for Facebook, Twitter, Google+, LinkedIn, or via email. All you have to do is click the one you want and they will tell the rest of the world (or your followers anyway) about your brand new service offering!

Also make sure to optimize the keywords for your gig. It is

better that they match the title of your gig, because this way they will have greater impact. Just like I recommended in the "YouTube" section use the Google Keyword Planner to determine the best keywords for your gig.

Step #7: Provide GREAT customer service.

Because Fiverr allows the buyers to rate you, you're going to want to be a true professional to them so that you get a higher score. Of course, you can't always please everyone, but the happier your clients are overall, the more work you'll get and the more money you'll make. There is a golden rule to Fiverr long term success "Just over deliver". Make sure that you surpass your buyer's expectations.

You can do so by applying a simple trick. For example if you are a writer and you want to offer to write articles, the usual word count for 5$ is between 300-500 words. If you are ok writing 500 words for 5$, you can offer in your gig 400 words for 5$, but always deliver around 500. This way the clients will be very pleased with your service and will come back.

Sometimes you will meet some bad buyers of course. Then you have to put your long term interests over and above your short term losses. They will be more demanding and pays less. Let a bad client go professionally and respectfully and focus on your good clients instead. Also never try to please a bad client, because you don't want a bad returning client.

Step #8: Learn from other Fiverr sellers.

One of the best ways to learn is to mirror what others are doing on Fiverr that seems to be working for them. Dion appears to be one of the top sellers, so you might want to check him out and see what he can teach you about what it takes to be a top seller like him!

EARNING POTENTIAL

You must start out at $5 per gig, be on the site at least 30 days, and complete a minimum of ten orders in order to start making real money on Fiverr. But if you are fast at what you do, you can earn a decent amount of spending cash off this particular site as long as you're comfortable working on a number of different projects in order to do so.

Some Fiverr members have reported earning hundreds of dollars a day, which is possible as long as you get a lot of gigs as a top seller or are able to sell add-ons. Members can make around $2,000 a month from Fiverr with for about 50 hours a month. This requires quite a time commitment to achieve, but it is possible if you're good at whatever it is you are selling and can get a lot of buyers to want your services.

8   SELLING PHYSICAL PRODUCTS ONLINE

Another way to earn money online is by selling physical products on sites like Amazon, Flipkart, eBay, etc. While you may not earn enough to make a living selling your own personal items (unless you are able to acquire a lot of goods at low costs and can turn them around quickly), you can also help others sell their things, thereby earning yourself a nice little commission in the process.

HOW TO GET STARTED

How do you get started selling? Here are a few simple steps:

Step #1: Find a product to sell.

Your first step to making this Internet option work is finding a product to sell. Fortunately, there are several ways to go about it. For instance, you can start by taking a look around your house and seeing what you have that you no longer want or need as selling your unwanted or unused items is a great way to get them out of your house without just sending them to the trash. The key to making a lot of money is to make sure they are still in good, if not excellent condition.

That being said, some people do sell broken things online as others may be buying them with the intent of fixing them and offering them for resale. So, in essence, nothing is off limits ("one man's junk is another man's treasure") as long as you are honest and market it accordingly.

A second option is to frequent yard and garage sales (and swap meets, flea markets, and antique sales), as sometimes you can find great deals there that you can resell online.

Whether the item you purchased is in great condition already or you have what it takes to refinish it, you can make a lot of money off other people's no longer wanted goods.

If you can find a really good deal at retail or even wholesale stores, you can also buy direct from them and resell the items at a higher price. Liquidation events, going out of business sales, and discontinued items are great for this purpose. Just be aware that buying items with the sole purpose of resale may require that you pay tax on them, so you may want to consult with an accountant before taking that route.

Good items to consider selling are ones that appeal to a niche market. Hobbyists like to find unique things online, making this one area that you can do really well in.

Still not sure what to sell? EBay has a Selling Inspiration House that can help you "find top-selling items in your home." Just pick a room, select an item, and it will tell you how much they are currently going for online.

Step #2: Pick a platform and create an account.

Now that you have something to sell, it is time to decide where it is you want to sell it. Two of the most notable sites are Amazon and eBay. However, you can also list your item on Craigslist (best for bigger items like cars and furniture).

Be sure to read each one carefully so you know up front what is required of you as a seller and how much commission they will take on the sale. Some charge you to a subscription fee as well, so you're going to want to check all of this out prior to signing up.

Whichever one you choose, you're going to have to create

an account in order to list and get paid. So, pick the one (or ones) that is best suited for you and the items you want to get rid of, and provide all of the requested information to create a complete account.

In order to get your money from them, you are also going to have to provide payment information. To keep your bank information private, you can always create a PayPal/Paytm/UPI account and accept payment that way. (PayPal does charge fees as well, so you may have to weigh that into the cost and whether or not it is worth it given what you are selling.)

A great way to figure out which site you prefer is to buy something from it before even placing your goods for sale. This way you get firsthand knowledge of how it works from the buyer's perspective, allowing you to take them into consideration when it comes to selling your goods online.

Step #3: Prepare your listing for optimal results.

To get good results on your listing, you want to include both benefits and features of your product. For example, features of a TV include screen size, resolution, and things like that, whereas benefits are being able to see the television clearer, having a flat- screen that doesn't take up too much room, and being able to see your favorite sports up close, almost as if you were there in person.

Your product description needs to be complete as well. The more information you provide about what it is you're selling, the easier it will be for people to determine if that is what they are looking for. Think like a buyer and include everything you would want to know if you were making the purchase yourself.

It helps to be familiar with jargon that is often used on popular selling sites. For example, BN stands for brand new and VTG means vintage. HTF represents a hard to find item and VGC tells the buyer it is in very good condition. If something is unique or distinct about your product, point it out. The more you can make your product a "one of a kind," the greater your chance of selling it.

Use keywords in your listing so that your product can be easily found by anyone searching for it. Not sure which ones to use? Consider what words you would use to search for the item and just use them. Include the brand if it is likely to make a difference.

Your product pictures (the more the better) need to be high quality. If they are fuzzy or too far away, you're not going to give prospective buyers a good feeling. Also, make sure the surrounding environment is good too because people like to buy from others who appear to take care of their things.

If you're stuck on any of these things, look up other people's listings and use them as templates to write yours. Just be sure to choose a top seller so that you know how to create an ad that sells, not one that doesn't get noticed.

Step #4: Set your price.

As far as price is concerned, this one may take a little bit of research. Google the item you are selling and see what others are getting for it. Before pricing yours though, you'll want to take into consideration its condition.

Depending on the site you intend to use, you can sell your item via traditional auction or by set price. Auction means that you sell to the highest bidder (and you may want to set a minimum price so you don't practically give it away) and set price means that you sell it to anyone that wants it for the price which you are selling it.

If you have a bunch of smaller items and don't want to price them for individual sale, you may want to group them together and sell them as a package. This may also entice a buyer as they will be getting several things for one standard rate.

An additional tip: some successful sellers offer free shipping as it catches people's attention. It's easy enough do as you just have to add this amount to your base price. The one caveat is that shipping isn't always going to be the same price as it is location dependent. So, you're going to want to keep this in mind if you choose to take this route.

Step #5: List your product on Amazon or Flipkart.

 When you decide to list your product, you'll want to time your listing so you get the most out of it. For example, if you only have a 10-day window, you may want to post your product on a Thursday so that it appears online for two full weekends, giving you more bangs for your buck.

Another factor to consider is whether your item is seasonal, or in high demand during certain times of the year. If this is the case, you may want to wait to sell it, drawing in the most money possible.

Step #6: Promote your product.

Share your product on your social media sites, website, in forums, or on any other Internet site you can think of to draw attention to it. You never know. Even if the people you're reaching out to have no interest in it, they might know someone who does and share it with them. It's a win-win!

These days Amazon, Flipkart are running paid promotion on their platform for better reach to customer. You can do that too.

Step #7: Make the deal.

Once you have a specific buyer, you're ready to close the deal. This is a great time to confirm things such as price and delivery, as well as answer any questions they may have.

This is also where you collect payment. It is very important that you do this prior to shipping your item so that you don't wind up sending it out and never getting the money, in return.

Step #8: Deliver your product.

You want to make sure your item arrives in the same condition it left you in, so you're going to want to pack it well. Do this by putting in extra padding to avoid unintentional breakage or damage by the shipping company. You can even go one step further and take pictures of your item as it is being packaged as well as the finished box to show what condition it was in when it left you.

Then ship it according to the site's requirements, being sure to get a tracking number and insurance if you want to be extra safe or the item is worth a lot of money. Having your buyer sign for it ensures that they received it, and it protects you from scammers who insist that it never arrived.

Step #9: Grow your product-based business.

In order to survive long-term and grow on sites like eBay, you need to get good feedback from the people that you sell to. Keep this in mind as every interaction you have with your customers has the potential to promote your business—or break it.

Staying in good contact with them every step of the way will help establish a good buyer/seller relationship. Check your email often and don't list things while you're going to be away for an extended period of time as it could look bad on you as a seller.

9 ECOMMERCE

If you are planning to engage in "e-commerce", to take your business online. So, you have to learn about laws and regulations about online business. Because different country have different set of rules, even different states have different rules and tax laws. E-commerce is a new way of doing business but in current market scenario after COVID-19 e-commerce business is very familiar to people.

Online business is "different", right?

Well, actually, no. Still you are going to sell products or services to your customers. In e-commerce business your customers have to visit your website and in physical shop your customer have to visit your physical store. In both scenario either you are selling offline or online, you still need the customers to visit your store (Either Online Store or Physical/Local Store) to order.

A major difference is that your physical store can only be seen by a small group of people, whereas your online business can be seen by the whole world.

For many businesses, this is truly an advantage, representing a wonderful opportunity.

When planning to go online, therefore, you should spend some time thinking about your product and exactly who your target market is, because this will be a crucial factor in determining whether your business is a success or a failure.

If you are going to open a shop in local area you have to invest on shop, decoration inventory and marketing. Same for online. Making an e-commerce website is not enough. Its actually like you're opened a shop and shutter is not open. Customer have no idea what you're doing. Same if you are opened an e-commerce site then you have to market your website in your desired customer location.

You have to analyse your target customer and then promote your business. What it is that you plan to market on your e-commerce enabled website, and who will want to buy it? Some products will, by their very nature, not be totally suited to a worldwide market. Like many products or services are not required by some group of people or culture.

Secondly, give very careful thought about how you will get your product to the customer. For example, if you were to make Water Purifier in Delhi (as one of my client companies does) there is absolutely no sense in trying to sell one purifier at a time to a customer in the USA, because of the cost of delivery and different market as they are using parts that is itself imported from USA.

So, if your product is bulky, heavy or imported, selling outside your area may not be practical.

Furthermore, you need to consider that, most countries

use the same Standard International Trade Classification codes for deciding on how much import duty to levy on a particular product, the actual duty to be paid varies from country to country, and such variations can (and will) lead to disputes.

This is not the fault client or his customer, nevertheless, the result was an unhappy customer, who obviously did not become a regular customer.

Likewise, if you plan on selling a service online, can that service be provided outside your local area in such a way that you still make money? Do you need to have one of your own staff actually work with the customer (in which case, you need to stay local) or can the work be easily subcontracted on a global basis? Would it be easy to find such a local subcontractor capable of supplying your advertised service in such a way that both you and the customer are happy? How much would such a subcontractor cost?

Unless you can get positive answers to all of these questions, then, again, it may pay you to keep your services local, rather than overreaching, in order to become a global player.

HOW TO GET STARTED

To create an e-commerce website or store you have to do some research work and do work step by step.

Here's what you need to do:

Step #1:

Decide what you want sell on your store. Either products or services or both.

Step #2:

Your number one priority is to come up with a domain name that suits you and is easy for your customer to remember and recognize. Something short and catchy will often do the trick, like Amazon, Flipkart, eBay, etc. who offer various types products. Also, don't try get too close to a well-known trademarked name in an attempt to get more followers or you could run into problems.

Now you are going to setting up your website on a self-hosting website such as Besolve, Hostgator, Bluehost, or Dreamhost, all of which have packages for less than $1 per month, remember that .com's often work the best as that is what most people are used to. At this point, in India .in is becoming more universal as well, so that is an option you may want to consider.

Step #3:

You also want to create a LOGO that is pleasing to your target market and consistent with your brand. Choose colors and graphics that are representative of your business, making it easy for your potential client base to tell who and what you are doing.

Step #4:

Start adding products or service categories wise, with Short and long description, Tags and Good quality images with alt text and in proper format with potential keywords so your products or services are easier to find. This involves creating a title that draws them in and writing description that engages with details about product or service to benefits them in some way, while still making sure that each part of your description has the keywords where they need to be. Also always format your description to look appealing and to be easier to read.

Step #5:

Create Return Policy, Shipping Rules & Policy and Privacy Policy for your website. You can find these policy online easily for FREE or some website can do it for you for a small amount.

Step #6:

Get Payment Gateway for online payment and integrate shipping service provider API. These days many companies are providing shipping services for startups without any upfront. They charging per package basis.

Step #7:

Publish some articles on blog of the website and remember article should be related to your products or services. One very important thing to remember is to post regularly. Get your readers used to seeing your articles so they feel like you're a trusted friend and make them look forward to your posts, as if you are a part of their everyday life. And if someone coming to your website definitely many visitors can see your products or service listing too.

Step #9:

Promote your website. Promote your website, products or services on other platforms (such as your web page, social media accounts like Facebook and Twitter, YouTube, etc.) to draw others to see it. Follow and post on other people's blogs, inspiring their curiosity to go to your website and check out what website is about.

Put a budget for paid promotion on Google AdWords,

Facebook, Instagram, LinkedIn, etc.

10 DROPSHIPPING

Dropshipping is a type of retailing where, instead of the retailer (meaning you) actually keeping the goods in stock at their own location, they instead pass the order, along with the shipment details from a customer, to a wholesaler. It is then the job of the wholesaler to dispatch the goods ordered directly to your customer for you. The great thing about this method is that not only do you not need to have a large warehouse for storing all the goods you are selling, but also you make a profit through the price you pay for it wholesale, and the price that you sell it to your customer for.

In fact, where dropshipping is concerned, you are actually acting as the middleman for the product that your customer receives and the manufacturer who produces it. This particular type of system is extremely beneficial to both small retail shops, as well as internet based stores, or those people who use mailing catalogs in order to generate sales for their companies. In fact, many customers who purchase their products in this way seem to not be too bothered that there is a delay between the time when the products are ordered and when they actually have them arrive.

But the biggest problem that is being addressed by dropshipping is that retailers no longer have to worry about controlling their inventory, as this is done for them by the wholesaler instead. Unfortunately, in a more traditional retail setting, the products a store owner orders will be ordered in bulk, and they will then need to be kept in a secure location until they can be displayed and sold. What this means is that you are adding costs to an already large budget, as you will need to have storage space available, along with hiring staff to maintain the storage area and ensure that the goods are ready for delivery to the store and to know what levels each product is at. You will also need to spend money investing in a good quality security system in order to prevent the goods from being stolen.

However, if you were to use dropshipping instead, then you do not need to retain a large stock of your inventory on site, and also you no longer needed to employ a large team of staff.

Also, you will find that a large number of manufacturers now find the idea of dropshipping as a good investment, as it is also lowering their costs as well. Plus they are gaining an additional sales person who they do not actually pay a wage to. They are also saving themselves money as they no longer need to arrange for the delivery of large quantities of their goods to a retailer, so they are cutting down on their handling and fuel costs this way.

Instead, they can use the more inexpensive shipping methods that are now readily available by using either IndianPost, DTDC, UPS, FedEx or a locally based delivery company to ensure that their products are delivered directly to the customer. Plus, as many manufacturers have spent vast amounts of money ensuring that their warehouses are completely secure, they know that their products are safe until the day that they are dispatched, rather than them sitting in the back room of some retailer's shop with very little or no security on the property.

Yet there are some drawbacks to running a dropshipping business, and these we will look at in more detail later on in this book. Through this book, we will provide you with how you need to get started in the business of dropshipping, along with what you will need and the benefits, as well as the drawbacks.

FIVE GOLDEN RULES TO DROPSHIPPING

If you want to ensure that your dropshipping business is profitable, there are a number of things you need to remember. In this chapter, we will look more closely at these five golden rules to ensure that you can run a profitable business.

In order to make your business as profitable as possible, you need to find a product which will sell in sufficient quantities, as well as one which will provide you with a good mark up, in order for it to be truly profitable. Therefore, it is important that you try to determine what the demand for the product is, and also what competition, if any, there is for this particular product. Also, if you can, take a look at what your competition is charging for it. You may find that some businesses will have a much lower profit margin than others, including you.

It is best when first starting out selling products using dropshipping, that you only sell a select few. Plus, also that those that you do select are related, or can be targeted and sold to the same market set. It is important that you do not try to sell every dropshipping product that you find, as this will help you concentrate more on marketing your goods, as well as keeping your own costs to a minimum.
Plus, you are more likely to make an impact in the market place as well.

Due to its increased popularity, it is important that you find a reputable dropshipper for your business. Unfortunately, over recent months there have been many scams that have come to light in this particular industry. Avoid those people who are offering to sell you lists of dropshippers for 100's of dollars, unfortunately many of these are middlemen who are posing as dropshippers themselves, and will then charge much more than you actually should be paying.

Remember, the whole idea of using dropshipping is to keep your costs down rather than raising them, but also still be able to make a profit at the end of the day.

Also, if you are able to, avoid the "turnkey" internet businesses which are willing to sell you a package of products, e-commerce and marketing for an exorbitant membership fee or charge you a monthly fee. These types of businesses, you will soon find, do not actually help, but rather hinder, and you will soon find that you are not making any profit whatsoever, while they are.

However, do not let what we have written above frighten you off, instead just be aware of these pitfalls. However, one of the best ways of finding a reputable dropshipper is through looking at such directories as "Chris Malta's Worldwide Brands". This provides you with a whole list of legitimate, as well as reputable, dropshippers that you may wish consider using.

You will still need to deal with the problems associated with back orders and returns. Unfortunately, not all the hassles associated with running a normal retail business can be eliminated from a business that is run online. There will be times when you find that a product your customer has ordered is not in stock, and so will not be available for dispatch immediately. Therefore, you will need to work out these matters with your dropshipper ahead of any of these problems occurring. This will then provide you with answers that you can provide to your customer should such an event occur.

Finally, it is important that you treat your business just like any other business, so do not spam people. Also, do not use either a personal or free web page address for your online store, and also ensure that you register the business in your country. It is also important that you register with the GST (In India) office so that you have a GST number…and be prepared to file taxes as per government rules.

As long as you start off by expecting that your business is going to make a decent profit, then the chances are that you will automatically see an increase in this.

REASONS FOR STARTING A DROPSHIPPING BUSINESS

If you are looking for one of the best opportunities to be had today for running a business from home, and cost little if anything to set up, then a dropship business is probably the answer for you. Not only can you run this business from the comfort of your own home, you will not have to worry about keeping large amounts of inventory in stock and you will not have to worry about getting the products shipped to your customers. Plus, you can still run this type of business while working in your normal day to day job. However, if the business really does get off the ground, then you can become a work from home mother or father instead.

In order to get your dropship business started, you will need either your own website, or you can sell your products on Amazon, Flipkart, eBay, etc. Then once an order is received and has been paid for by a customer, you send the order over to your dropship supplier and they then send the order directly to your customer while you still make a profit. Also, you will need to set up an electronic payment system such as those provide by PayTm, PayPal, PayU, RazorPay, etc.

If you were to carry out a search of the web today, you will be amazed at the number of people who are making money through a dropshipping business. There are even some who are actually earning a 6 figure salary from theirs, and others who are just doing it part time in order to earn a little extra cash to provide them with a better way of life. In fact, many people often start their dropshipping business as a part time business, and it is only after the business has really taken off do they decide to do it full time instead.

The great thing about setting up dropshipping business is you do not need any special skill sets in order to get it started. All it really needs is a person who is willing to dedicate their time to ensure that the business succeeds, as well as having a computer and this being connected to the internet.

But the first thing you need to do once you decide to set up a dropshipping business is to form a good relationship with your dropship supplier. Once this has been formed, then you can start selling their products online, either through your own website, or on one of the many sites such as Amazon.

What you are actually doing is acting as a middleman and bringing together those who want to buy a particular product and those that are selling it, while still collecting a profit for you. The greatest benefit to be had from setting up this type of business is that you do not have to worry about inventory or paperwork as with a normal retail business, as this is all the worry of your dropship supplier instead.

The other great thing about setting up a dropshipping business is that you should find yourself almost making money instantly. If not today then tomorrow or the next day, but it certainly will not be long before you should start to see your first profits.

All you need to do is find a product that you feel people will buy, find a reputable dropship supplier, and then start advertising the product on Amazon. By using this method, you will find it costs very little in order to get your business up and running.

However, as with any business, it is best that you ensure that the products you are supplying are of the best quality possible, and also provide the best customer service that you can. So if you are selling your products through an auction site, then make sure you keep in touch with what is happening. If any of your customers have a question, then make sure that you respond as quickly as possible and follow up afterwards to ensure that they are satisfied with the information you provided to them.

Also, always select products that there are not thousands of them selling on the internet. By doing this, your business will not only be much more fun, but will also be much more profitable. So before you start selling any products through a dropshipping business, you should do as much research as possible first. Look for those products which have not saturated the market, or that has very few people competing for the customers, and therefore, the sales.

But what you do need to remember is that starting a dropshipping business is very easy, and you can run it from anywhere, especially out of your own home. Also, such a business can be run from anywhere in the world, and will cost you very little in getting it started.

THINGS TO CONSIDER

As you will soon discover, dropshipping is an extremely effective business model for anyone who wants to start an online retail business. You can either run it through your own website, or through some other outlet, such as an auction site.

However, due to this form of online business has become so easy to do, and because of its increased popularity, many prospective dropshipping businesses have become targets for the less reputable people online, such as scammers.

Unfortunately, many people who do not really understand what dropshipping is about only see it as a way of getting rich quick. Because of this, there are plenty of people out there who are ready to exploit them. In this article, we will look more closely at the things you should consider before you decide to go ahead and set up a dropshipping business for   yourself.

1. You need to carry out plenty of research with regard to dropship sources. It is best if you avoid using search engines when doing this, as they will also offer up a list of the less reputable companies around, as well as providing you with page upon page of links which are completely useless. However, once you have found a reputable source for the information that you require, and then the real work begins.

2. Avoid any companies which expect you to pay them an up-front fee (membership or monthly). Also avoid those which offer you a fully featured dropshipping solution that provides you with a website and everything else that you need in order to get your business off the ground.

3. Ensure the dropshippers you are looking at require a valid wholesale certificate from you. You will gain this through a business license,

so avoid any that don't have that requirement at all costs. Unfortunately, most of the companies which are willing to do business with an illegal business will usually be middlemen, who then send your order through to the wholesale company, and will end up taking a cut of the profits that you are trying to make.

The best way to find a legitimate dropshipping company is as follows:-

    a.   If you have seen a product which you are interested in selling, then contact the company producing it direct. Enquire if they have a dropshipping facility, and if they don't, then they are likely to be a light bulk seller. This means that they will only normally sell their products wholesale with a minimum of say around $200 or so (in many cases, the minimum number is much higher).

    b.   Another way is looking at such directories that have been set up and deal directly with legitimate dropshipping companies only. One such directory is Worldwide Brands. Such directories offer you an extensive searchable list of products, and which companies supply them. So if you are looking for a way to save yourself time in searching for good quality products to sell through your online business, then these directories are certainly the right way to go.

4.   However, once you have found a company that does offer dropshipping facilities; you will need to get a valid reseller/wholesale

certificate. Yet, what the exact requirements are in order for you to obtain this certificate will vary from state to state. But the minimum requirement for starting any dropshipping business online is that you have a business license.

5. Now you need to contact the dropshipping company in question and set up an account with them. Unfortunately, you may find that because your business is new, and you are not able to supply any references, then you may find that you need to set up a pre-paid account with them. Normally, this means that they will charge your purchases to a credit card instead of providing you with a line of credit. In order for this to be done, you will need to fill out a credit card form, an account application and provide them with your wholesale certificate. Once this has been received, they will then provide you with a wholesale catalog and anything else that you need in order to get your business up and running with their products.

6. Also, do not be fooled by those sites offering you a dropship directory for a fee (normally around $5 to $15). Unfortunately, these are normally copies of the more legitimate lists provided by reputable directories, and will often be out of date. So really, you are better off going to one of the more reputable directories and paying them a little extra in order to get a regularly updated list.

7. Now that you have found the product which you are interested in selling, and you have made arrangements with the dropshipper in question, it is time to get your site up and running, or your account set up with one of

the more reputable auction sites, such as eBay.

THE ADVANTAGES AND DISADVANTAGES

Although dropshipping today is a very hot topic being discussed among many retailers, and it does have many benefits, it may not be the best option for every business. However, in this chapter we will take a closer look at some of the advantages, as well as disadvantages to be had from running an online dropshipping business.

First, if you are just starting out in setting up an online business, and do not have much operating capital, then this may be the best option for you to go with. The great thing about this particular type of business is that you do not need to hold vast stocks of the products that you are selling. Instead, this is all done for you by the dropshipping supplier you have gone into partnership with. This results in you eliminating a significant cost in order for your business to be set up and to get it running.

The site you set up can be produced very quickly, and so be providing the product to those people you are targeting.

As you are getting the customers' orders before you actually order the goods from the supplier, this means that you have little or no initial investment to make.

Because you are not actually holding any of the inventories yourself, then you do not need to pay either for storage facilities, or having to invest in expensive merchandise which you may not in fact sell.

Setting up an online dropshipping business provides you with the chance to diversify what you are actually offering to your customers. In fact, you will only be limited by not being able to find the right dropshipper for the product or items that you wish to sell.

Although there are plenty of advantages to setting up a dropshipping business, there are many disadvantages as well.

First, as you do not own the inventory that you are selling, then you will usually find that you have no control on how the product is packaged. Also, you will not be able to include any coupons or offers in to the package which can help in increasing the amount of return business you get.
Every company which offers their dropshipping services will have a different fee structure, so carry out as much in depth research as possible. In fact, you do not want to end up with high shipping costs, as this will only make people less reluctant to purchase their goods from you.

With dropshipping, because you are only ordering one item at the time rather than bulk amounts, then you will not expect to get the same kinds of discounts.

If you decide to sell multiple products that are supplied by multiple dropshipping companies, then you will also see a significant increase in the fees that you pay to the dropshippers, which, in turn, will need to be passed onto your customer in order for you to make a profit.

There are many suppliers who will be able to provide you with dropshipping services that you can use to integrate their products into your website.
However, you may find that you will be charged a fee for using a particular service through them, so be sure that you carry out your research thoroughly before opting for one particular dropship supplier.

One major drawback to be had from setting up a dropshipping business is that not all manufacturers allow for dropshipping. This is because they will need to employ more staff (extra costs) in order for them to process these individual orders, and could result in delays in their normal shipping and receiving system.

There are other companies who will only supply in bulk, so this means that it is impossible for smaller outlets to get custom orders provided for them for select numbers of items.

However, when dropshipping is available, certainly many small as well as internet based businesses find that it can solve many more problems than those it may create.

HOW TO GET STARTED

It really is very easy to get your dropshipping business up and running. The main pieces of equipment that you will need are a good computer, and also a good quality internet connection.

But not only is it fairly easy to get your business up and running, you will find that there are very few barriers which will prevent you from getting started, and the cost for starting out is very low, so you should not need to invest much money up front initially.

However, below these are the steps that you will need to take in order to get your dropshipping business up and running.

Step #1:

Set yourself up an online shop, either using one of the many online shop builder programs available, or by building your own site, or setting up an account with an auction site such as eBay (if you choose to use eBay as your primary selling place, I recommend getting a good auction template that you can simply plug your information into to save time).

Step #2:

Find your wholesale supplier who has the product that are looking to sell, and who offers a dropshipping service.

Step #3:

Once you have found the company that you want to deal with, you can open an account with them.

Step #4:

Next thing you need to do is start building your site, using both content and images that the dropshipping supplier has provided, or that you have produced yourself (I recommend the latter, as it will distinguish you from other sellers who may be utilizing the same dropshipper).

Step #5:

Set up a system on your site so that you know when an order has been placed for a particular item, and so payment can be taken.

Step #6:

Pass on the details of the order directly to your dropshipping supplier. Once they receive the order, they will then bill you at the price that you have both agreed upon, and then they will arrange for the item to be dispatched. In most cases, the dropshipping supplier will provide labels which refer to the business or website where the order has come from, rather than from their own business.

As you can see from above, setting up a dropshipping business is an excellent way to get started with an online business, and if done correctly, should not be an expensive project.

As you will soon discover, there are hundreds of companies who are willing to provide dropship products to you. Whether it is gifts of items for the home, to power tools and furniture, the choices are immense.

Certainly, dropshipping will offer you many advantages if you are only starting up an online business with very little or no capital. One of the main ones being that the product you are selling does not need to be paid for until it is actually sold, and as you are paid for it by the customer, then the outlay you make to the dropshipper supplier is nothing.

Along with not having to make any outlay to the supplier in order for the product to be sold on your site, you also do not have to worry about storage and handling costs, as this is all covered for you by the dropship supplier you are using.

Plus, by setting up a site where your goods are supplied to you by a dropship supplier, you can offer a much wider variety of items, from a number of different suppliers, and your customers will never know any different.

Unfortunately, there are some downsides to running a dropshipping business, and the main ones are that you do not have any control over the inventory management, whether the product is readily available and if the orders can be fulfilled and shipped on time to the customer who has ordered them.

But if you are still interested in setting up a dropshipping business in order to earn an extra income online, then carry out as much research as possible.

The best thing of all is that, when setting up such a business, it does not need to be expensive or time consuming.

CONCLUSION

Making money online or grow your business online is possible and you now have the viable options from which to choose. Try one or try them all and see which one suits you, your home life, and your desired outcome best.

These can be your hobbies or interest which can produce incomes capable of supporting you and your family easily (such as mobile apps and SEO). But none of them will work unless you put the time and effort into them that they require.

There is no such thing as easy money; there is only becoming more efficient and effective so that it comes to you faster and with less effort. Hopefully now it will.

ABOUT THE AUTHOR

Qais Raza is the founder and Director of Besolve Solutions Private Limited, is a renowned software development company. Qais Raza is a first generation entrepreneur and incorporates his unique background as a technical person, and senior executive with BESOLVE into a transformational relationship with his clients.